MW00657509

RELATIONSHIPS
THAT WORK

RELATIONSHIPS
THAT WORK

The Power of Conscious Living

How Transformative Communication
Can Change Your Life

DAVID B. WOLF, PH.D.

MANDALA
PUBLISHING
San Rafael, CA

Mandala Publishing
17 Paul Drive
San Rafael, CA 94903
www.mandala.org
800.688.2218

© 2008 David B. Wolf. All rights reserved. No part of this book may be reproduced in any form without permission from the publisher.

Library of Congress Cataloging-in-Publication Data available.

ISBN-10: 1-60109-015-3
ISBN-13: 978-1-60109-015-7

Palace Press International, in association with Roots of Peace, will plant two trees for each tree used in the manufacturing of this book. Roots of Peace is an internationally renowned humanitarian organization dedicated to eradicating land mines worldwide and converting war-torn lands into productive farms and wildlife habitats. Together, we will plant two million fruit and nut trees in Afghanistan and provide farmers there with the skills and support necessary for sustainable land use.

Printed in China by Palace Press International
www.palacepress.com

10 9 8 7 6 5 4 3 2 1

The content of this book is provided for informational purposes only and is not intended to diagnose, treat, or cure any conditions without the assistance of a trained practitioner. If you are experiencing a medical condition, seek care from an appropriate licensed professional.

Table of Contents

A Note from the Author

An integral element of my life purpose and service to the world is sharing the principles and skills of transformative communication with you. I have a deep conviction that the application of these spiritual principles and strategies will profoundly enhance your life and relationships. My experience with people and my personal challenges to integrate spiritual wisdom consistently confirm the power of conscious living and the universality of the paradigms, perspectives and tools in this book. Whoever you are, spirit-based principles of personal growth and the techniques of conscious communication will work for you. My hope is that this book will be a seed that flowers in your life, producing ever more savory fruits of soulful fulfillment and relationship satisfaction.

Relationships that work begin with the relationship with our self. On the first page we distinguish the self from the body. To cite Teilhard de Chardin, "We are not human beings having a spiritual experience. We are spiritual beings having a human experience." The process of reading this book is meant to facilitate a connection with your authentic spiritual personality—the spiritual core that is not defined by any role you play or possessions attached to your name. As confirmed by the great wisdom traditions, this spiritual consciousness is the foundation for a life of peaceful existence, powerful vision and purposeful action.

Living from truly spiritual consciousness, our qualities of compassion, vitality and love naturally radiate. Sharing confidences with others is a heartfelt way to exchange affection. Such exchange engenders change, as we embody genuine love by supporting and challenging each other to grow. Love is the greatest wealth, and like material wealth it can multiply. Cultivate mastery of the methods of transformative communication and you will possess the currency to express the richness of your soul in every situation and to create relationships that work.

PART ONE

Spiritual Principles
of Personal Growth

Who Am I?

Expressions such as awakening, enlightenment, self-improvement and personal development have become household words. But what do they really mean? What is it that awakens or enlightens? What is the self that improves? Who is the one that develops?

Through science we know that the body continuously changes and transforms itself. Not one cell in your body now was part of your five-year-old body. Yet when you look at a childhood photo you think, "That is me when I was five," although the body is completely different. So how do we recognize ourselves? Clearly there is something that remains the same, apart from bodily and even mental changes. This something indicates an identity separate from the body and mind, an unchanging spiritual essence. It is to this spiritual essence that the world's wisdom traditions point.

The focal point for spiritual principles of personal growth is our true identity beyond the physical body and subtle mind. To be satisfying and complete, our self-help endeavors must recognize this non-physical self. It is common to lose connection with this essential self, even without realizing we have done so. Søren Kierkegaard once stated, "The greatest danger, that of losing one's own self, may pass off quietly as if it were nothing; every other loss, that of an arm, a leg, five dollars, a wife, is sure to be noticed."

Athato brahma jijnasa. This well-known Sanskrit aphorism helps me to remember my spiritual identity, and purpose in life. The meaning of the adage is "Now is the time to inquire into the nature of Ultimate reality." It signifies that now that we possess a human form of life, we have a responsibility to deliberate about spiritual matters. There is some obvious importance to fulfilling the needs of the body, such as eating, sleeping and shelter. However, if our inquiries and endeavors do not extend beyond that, then we are not realizing the capacity of our spirit. If I buy an expensive computer and use it as a doorstop, it will not fulfill its actual potential. Just as the computer can accomplish much more than stopping a door, so we too can use our bodies, mind and intelligence to elevate our consciousness for the purpose of spiritual progress.

Since the word "spiritual" is used in a variety of ways, it is important to define my understanding of the term. By spiritual I mean *beyond, or not limited by, materially based identifications*—such as "I am thin," "I am the mother of this child," "I look great in a suit," "I am a member of this religion" or "I am a very disciplined person." These appellations apply to the covering of the spirit self, but not to the actual self.

I drive a Toyota. Naturally I care for the car, keeping it tuned up and filled with the right fluids. But if I think that my own thirst is quenched when I fill the car with gasoline, I am under an illusion and will not be satisfied. I do not believe that I am Japanese just because the car was made in Japan, any more than I would believe myself to be German if I were driving a Mercedes-Benz. Clearly this is a foolish idea. Yet if we identify with designations that apply to the temporary body (the vehicle) rather than the spiritual self, we are making the same mistake. Just as the owner of the car changes to another car when the old one is finished, our spirit changes to another body at the time of death. Recognizing and attending to material designations or roles may serve the spiritual journey, just as an automobile can facilitate travel to the destination. But misidentification of the self with these designations is a diversion from our pursuit of spiritual understanding. It often leads to many unhealthy *isms*, such as nationalism, sexism and racism.

Bodies change, spiritual identity remains. Thoughts also change. Some bring a smile to our face, others are embarrassing. Some are practical, some are outlandish. But *we* are not our thoughts. So what is the nature of this thing that thinks, that uses fingers to write with a keyboard, that peers through eyes that read, "So what is the nature of this thing that thinks..."?

THE NATURE OF SPIRIT

Great wisdom traditions affirm that our nature reflects the supreme. In Genesis, for example, it is said that we are created in the image of God. What is this supreme nature that we represent? Is it fearful? Confused? Resentful? Weak? Overwhelmed with anxiety? When I think of divine nature, I envision qualities such as power, vitality, fearlessness, contentment and compassion. In accord with the world's major wisdom traditions, my conviction is that our fundamental nature is spiritual and sacred, inherently balanced, whole and complete. This understanding underlies the principles and process of this book.

The Vedic body of spiritual knowledge that has inspired much of my thought describes the central qualities of our spirit as *sat*, *chit* and *ananda*. This means that we are constitutionally *eternal*, *conscious* and *blissful*. We can understand something about this nature by observing ourselves. For example, whether through anti-lock brakes or thermonuclear devices, much of our energy is employed in eluding death. Why? Because as spiritual beings we are not meant to die. Each of us seeks to expand our consciousness, perhaps through a study of history, philosophy, or maybe through the politics and economics of the day. We strive for happiness, knowledge, and eternity in so many ways, but often do not find the joy and fulfillment we seek. This indicates that our activities may be misdirected with respect to spiritual development, and leads us to wonder, "What is my essential activity as a spiritual being?"

SERVICE AS OUR DHARMA

To enrich understanding of our innate spiritual qualities, the principle of dharma is very helpful. Dharma refers to "that which cannot be separated from a thing." Fire, for example, can be used for different purposes, such as cooking. Cooking however is not the dharma of fire, because fire can exist without cooking. *Heat* is the dharma of fire. Heat is an intrinsic, inseparable quality of fire.

From observation we can understand that our dharma is to serve. As sugar cannot avoid being sweet, so we too cannot avoid serving. It is our constitutional nature. Where there is a human being, there is service. We may direct our propensity for service in different directions; perhaps we serve our nation, family or company, our belly, an ideology or our species. The way in which we manage our propensity to serve will greatly influence our experiences of life, and of ourselves.

If our inherent tendency to serve is applied only toward bodily functions, the spiritual self is left empty. Being spiritual, our nature is spiritual service. Spiritual service means that our endeavors enhance the spiritual lives of ourselves and others. One important principle of personal growth is to be a source for the spiritual development of others. Service is the natural activity that evokes the joy of the soul.

For our service to be complete and satisfying, it needs to address the spirit—the driver of the car. Spiritual growth is not an exercise in self-absorption; it involves determined dedication to the highest aspirations of others. We can think of our spiritual core as the root of the tree of our being. Just as watering or serving the root automatically nourishes all parts of the tree, attending to our spirit nurtures each dimension of our selves—including the physical, intellectual, emotional and social. Truly being of service to others means relating to them as essentially spiritual in nature.

EXAMINING ASSUMPTIONS

Throughout this book you will have the opportunity to examine assumptions by which you live your life. Awareness of our assumptions, or belief systems, enables us to consider whether they actually work for us. It also allows us to be open to alternative, more satisfying possibilities for viewing ourselves and the world. Being conscious of our assumptions helps us to take responsibility for changing them, or purposefully utilizing them—rather than letting our belief systems determine our lives from beneath the conscious surface.

Already I have shared some of my assumptions, including the conviction that we are inherently spiritual persons whose nature it is to serve. Another assumption I embrace is that each of us possesses the capacity to handle his or her life with a high level of effectiveness. This is consistent with the understanding of the intrinsic qualities of the self described above. In expressing our innate qualities we are able to produce extraordinary results in our lives. The process of spiritual growth described in this book is meant to serve as testimony to this assumption.

Presuppositions can filter our perception of reality, often preventing us from accessing our facility for conscious choice. Let us take a look at how this process conceals awareness.

I recall an experiment in an undergraduate cognitive psychology class. We, the approximately two-dozen students, were the subjects. The professor showed us a film about a minute long of a staged robbery on a city street. Afterwards each student completed a questionnaire of twenty closed-ended items. The questions dealt with details of the movie crime we had just witnessed, including items such as *Did the robber have a gun?*, *Did the robbery victim hold her purse in her left hand?* and *Did you notice a bakery on the street?* Next to each *yes* or *no* response we indicated whether we were *not sure* or *sure* about that response, and, if we were sure, whether we would be willing to give this response under oath in court. After again viewing the film and tallying the results we found that every person in the class had been willing to testify to at least one lie.

Look at the phrases in the triangles below.

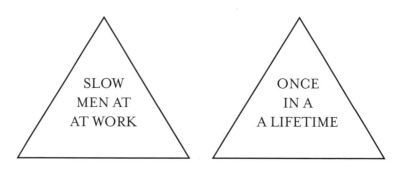

SLOW
MEN AT
AT WORK

ONCE
IN A
A LIFETIME

Read aloud what they say.

Now look again at the triangles and phrases. Again, read aloud what you see.

If you read SLOW MEN AT WORK and ONCE IN A LIFETIME, read again, because that is not what is written. This time, as you read, point to each word.

What do the phrases actually say?

Do you notice the sentences read "SLOW MEN AT _AT_ WORK" and "ONCE IN A _A_ LIFETIME"?

When seeing the phrases the first, second and even the third time, most people don't read what is actually there. We miss what is there because we are conditioned to assume what must be written. Unexamined assumptions, instead of facilitating our under-standing of reality, serve as a barrier to a fresh experience of reality. We can extend this understanding to our lives, where we often do not experience a situation as it actually is, or a person as he or she is, because we have already assumed how it must be, or what he or she must be like.

This book describes an approach to communication and spiritual empowerment that assists you in conscious living, in living life intentionally, not accidentally. You will be able to determine whether you are living life out of unconscious habit, or whether you are consciously choosing this way of being and acting because it genuinely works for you.

Exercise

Below are nine dots arranged in a set of three rows. Recreate these dots on a separate sheet of paper. The challenge is to connect all nine dots, using four straight lines, starting from any dot, without lifting your pen or pencil from the paper. Lines may cross, though you cannot retrace any lines. Lines must pass through the middle of all the dots, and each line must start where the previously drawn line finished.

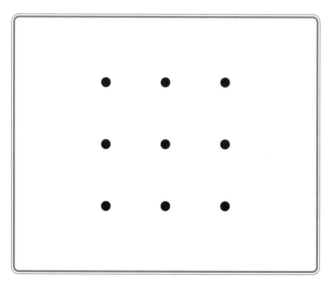

Do not look at the answer (page 10) until you have either found a solution that meets all the guidelines described above or you have given up. Do not give up too easily. Try it for at least five minutes.

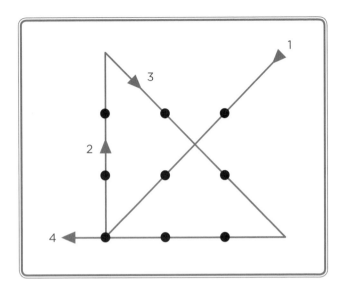

When I give this exercise in my seminars, on average about five percent of people quickly find the solution. If it took you a while to discover the solution, or if you needed to look at the answer, consider what assumptions prevented you from arriving at the solution.

Most of us assume that the solution must lie within the dots—as if there is some boundary around the nine dots. But the instructions don't say anything about whether we must stay within the dots or whether we can venture *outside*. If we assume that the solution lies within the dots, it is impossible to solve. Within the framework of our assumptions, it is not possible. Some people though intuitively assume that the solution lies outside the boundary of the dots, and for them the solution is easy.

You are probably familiar with the term *thinking outside the box*, and perhaps many of us regard ourselves as outside-the-box thinkers. The nine-dots exercise indicates the extent to which we instinctively think outside the box.

This game is an example where a certain set of assumptions proves futile. No matter how hard we worked within that worldview, our efforts were unsuccessful. Only by expanding our boundaries and challenging our self-imposed limitations could we become effective. This game is a metaphor for the process of spiritual transformation. To grow we need to examine our assumptions, about ourselves, our relationships, abundance and every aspect of existence. This process involves challenging the limitations of our worldview, and our view of what is possible for us to achieve. Frequently those limitations are composed of self-created conceptions and perceptions. Perceptions are powerful. They create restrictions as well as opportunities, as demonstrated in some real-life examples described below that illustrate success in thinking without self-imposed limitations.

Cliff Young was a potato farmer and sheepherder. In 1983, at the age of sixty-one, he entered the 544-mile ultra-marathon from Sydney to Melbourne, although he lacked any racing experience. Cliff was quite a sight in his overalls and galoshes, in contrast to the running uniforms of the many world-class runners who participated in the event. Cliff, regarded as a laughingstock and some sort of mental case, fell far behind on the first day.

For Cliff to make it through the first day of the race would have been impressive. To complete the entire race would have been considered incredible. Not only did Cliff finish the race, he won. Not only did he win, but he won by a day-and-a-half.

The highly trained and experienced runners, several of them legendary in their sport, knew that the best way to complete the six-day event was to run for eighteen hours, rest for six, and then resume running. Cliff was clueless about this unquestioned strategy, though, and just kept running through the night. (Since then, runners have come to understand that to win the race you have to run night and day.) Other runners needed to *unlearn* what they thought they knew, in order to transcend self-imposed constraints. As Mark Twain said, "It's not what I don't know that limits me. It's what I know that ain't so."

Cliff Young was not thinking inside the box, nor was he thinking outside the box. For him there was no box. Allow your experience of this book to be an opportunity to consider perspectives and possibilities that you may be missing due to attachment to a fixed worldview. Awareness of self-limiting beliefs weakens their ability to run our lives, and creates possibilities for breakthrough results and experiences. This can translate as relationship satisfaction that we did not consider possible, abundance we didn't believe to be available, a level of health previously thought unattainable or unimagined spiritual fulfillment.

Perhaps you are familiar with the story of the four-minute mile. It used to be considered an unreachable goal for a human being. In 1954, Roger Bannister ran a mile in under four minutes. Within a year thirty-seven runners had done the same; within two years 300 runners had accomplished this feat. The barrier was not physical. It was a barrier of belief.

What are some belief barriers that you are holding onto? Identify what you are telling yourself—about yourself, about life, about commitment, wealth, and happiness—that prevents you from full achievement. It is a principle of creation that things go from subtle to gross. (For example, any invention begins subtly, with thought.) Change begins in the world of ideas. What is happening externally is a reflection of what is happening internally. Shining the light of awareness on what is going on inside uncovers creative potential that has been locked away.

Examples of belief barriers in the area of abundance could include "Rich people are cheaters," "If I am wealthy I can't be spiritual," and "If I have a lot of money I will lose my friends." Now, I don't want to be a cheater, I like to think of myself as spiritual, and I want friends. So if these thoughts are going on inside me, then despite my efforts to improve my financial situation, I will sabotage myself. Perhaps I am maintaining beliefs such as "I am not trustworthy," "I am not lovable," or "I am powerless." Because subtle thoughts lead to gross manifestation, I will create situations that confirm my sense of not being trustworthy, lovable or powerful.

Looking squarely and concretely at what we are saying to ourselves permits us to change that inner conversation and transform our lives. French novelist Marcel Proust wrote, "The real act of discovery consists not in finding new lands but in seeing with new eyes." If we are rigidly set in our paradigms (sets of interrelated assumptions that form the way we perceive reality and relate to the world), we may not recognize potential breakthroughs available to us.

Much of this book focuses on changing our experience of life through transforming our communication with others. However, transformative communication begins with awareness and metamorphosis of our communication *with ourselves*. Exploration of belief barriers is observation of self-communication. In following the process described in this book you will learn principles, strategies and tools to transform this inner talk and profoundly alter your experience of self and the world.

There are numerous examples where "new eyes," or an alternate perspective, has fostered groundbreaking discovery. In the 1930s, Chester Carlton invented a device that produced photographic images using a specially coated metal plate, bright light and a fine black powder. His supervisor at Kodak Company was not interested in this innovative way of creating images, and did not encourage Carlton's endeavors. Carlton, however, persisted. The Xerox company, with a fresh perspective, went on to develop this method for electrostatic photography, and in 1948 introduced the world's first photocopier.

In the late sixties, Swiss watchmakers enjoyed 65 percent of the world market share. Then Swiss researchers invented a fully electronic, battery-operated quartz-movement watch, more accurate than conventional mechanical watches. Watch manufacturers in Switzerland, however, didn't believe that this represented the future of timepieces. Japanese manufacturers acquired the technology from the Swiss, and soon the market was flooded with digital watches. Within a decade Swiss market share had plunged to less than 10 percent.

Not seeing beyond our axiomatic assumptions can be costly. A coaching client once described her realization that while she was in a certain relationship, she wasn't able to see her boyfriend for who he was. Rather, she saw him through her assumptions, her set of expectations of *how she believed he should be*. "I had this idea, I just assumed it was true, that because of him our relationship wasn't working. I was constantly looking at him to find the source of our problems. He had to change; he was never really okay in my eyes. My way of thinking was infectious. At one point he even told me that he's not good enough for me, just like I'd been projecting onto him. I broke up with him. Now I'm seeing with completely different eyes. I realize that I don't see myself as good enough. How I was treating him was about what I sense is lacking in me."

The above examples illustrate the value in examining our assumptions about life. In the process described in these pages you are invited to explore assumptions you hold in each area of your life, and how well they work for you. To effect profound personal change through this process involves being open and willing to learn. This book provides a structure consisting of principles, skills, and processes to inspire progress in whatever domain you choose. Our sets of assumptions constitute our conditioning for relating to the world, our box for thinking, feeling, and acting. Next, we will examine various paradigms of consciousness that form our underlying approach to existence.

BE-DO-HAVE

*"First say to yourself what you would be;
and then do what you have to do."*

— Epictetus

I conduct transformative communication and self-empowerment seminars. These seminars provide an environment for spiritually based personal development. During one part of the training we ask participants what are some tangible, material things for which people strive. Typically the resulting list looks something like this: cars, computers, a big house, an attractive spouse, children, job, jewelry, insurance, and vacation time. Then we ask why people strive for such things. This second list commonly includes experiences such as happiness, security, power, intimacy, fulfillment, balance, love, vitality, freedom, strength, courage, joy, and affection.

Next, by observing the two lists we consider whether there are persons who possess a large house, a big car, and a prestigious job, but who do not experience much joy, power, or fulfillment in their lives. Certainly there are. Then we consider whether there are persons who experience an abundance of happiness, intimacy, and vitality in their lives, although they don't have the items on the other list. Clearly such persons exist. The conclusion is that there is no intrinsic connection between the two lists. Although they sometimes overlap, there is no inherent causal link.

Three Modes of Nature

According to the Vedas—the spiritual literature of ancient India—three *gunas*, or modes of material nature, permeate all facets of existence, from psychology to diet, from work to recreation. With reference to the three *gunas*, let's explore the lack of innate correlation between the *things* list and the *experience* list.

Tamas is the mode of *inertia*, where our consciousness clings to a worldview that could be called Have-Do-Be. In this worldview we think, "If I could just *have* $100,000 in the bank, a nicer car, a job with paid vacation, then I could *do* what I want to do, and then I will *be* happy, satisfied, appreciated, vibrant." Or, "If I *had* a nicer boss, then I would *be* content and peaceful." In this mindset our experience is dependent on having. The adage "What profits a man if he gains the whole world yet loses his soul?" indicates the difficulties this attitude may bring.

Rajas is the mode of activity where we adhere to the framework of Do-Have-Be. In this way of thinking I consider that if I could just *do* what I want to do, then I will *have* what I want, and then I will *be* free, strong, giving and vital. In this scenario our consciousness starts from the point of activity, and experience is contingent upon that. With reference to this paradigm, Bhaktivedanta Swami writes: "Out of ignorance only, less intelligent persons try to adjust to the situation by fruitive activities, thinking that resultant actions will make them happy." This is the To Do list model of existence. "If I could just complete my To Do list, I would be peaceful, content, and satisfied." In reality, it rarely works out that way. We are not human *doings*. We are human *beings*.

Sattva guna corresponds with enlightenment. *Sattvic* consciousness is the natural state of the authentic self. Steady in *sattva*, we live in the worldview of Be-Do-Have. Fixed in this way of being, experiencing strength, beauty, balance, security, intimacy, warmth, and freedom is not dependent on doing or having. I don't need to do or have anything to experience satisfaction, aliveness, courage, and clarity—because these qualities are who I am. They are my essential nature. It is important to note that the Be-Do-Have worldview does not lack doing and having. In fact, our doing and having assume full potency, contrasted with *tamasic* or *rajasic* perspectives, because what we do and have flow naturally from our being. They are not separate endeavors. To experience joy, closeness, radiance and all other qualities of our self is not dependent on what we do or have. In Be-Do-Have, we naturally do things that bold, enlivened, successful people do, because our nature is bold, enlivened, and successful. And of course we will have things that powerful, confident, and trusting people have—such as abundance, rewarding activity, and fulfilling relationships.

The well-known sacred text *Bhagavad Gita*, presenting the essence of Vedic teachings, delineates a Be-Do-Have approach to life. In this book Lord Krishna encourages his friend Arjuna to "Be transcendental... be free from dualities, be without anxiety, and be established in the self." For many years I had been intrigued by the philosophical and psychological model described in the *Gita*. During my doctoral program I researched its systematic explanation of the *gunas* as a paradigm for understanding the incredible diversity we find in people and the world. This investigation resulted in the development of the Vedic Personality Inventory (VPI), a statistically validated personality assessment based on the paradigm of the three *gunas*. This research confirms the Vedic assertion that *sattvic* practices and attitudes correlate with greater fulfillment, balance and life satisfaction. The VPI is included in Appendix A, and I encourage you to complete it when you finish this section of the book to provide a baseline of your present relationship with the three modes of nature.

Be-Do-Have Applied

One of my coaching clients and I once focused specifically on him being patient and peaceful—qualities that were missing in his life, and which he wanted to cultivate. With earnest effort he connected with the patience and calm inherent to his being. During our following coaching session, he described with surprise that his supervisor had asked him to accept a position with increased responsibility, involving training others. The supervisor particularly mentioned that she offered the promotion because of his patience and his ability to remain calm in stressful situations. Being patient and peaceful naturally resulted in acting in ways that patient and peaceful people act (in this instance a more rewarding career activity), and having things that patient and peaceful people have (in this example an increased income). That's Be-Do-Have.

In the above example we refer to "qualities that were missing." Actually patience and peacefulness were never missing. They were covered. A diamond is always brilliant, radiant and strong, though it can be covered by dust or mud. Similarly, we never lose our qualities, though we may allow them to be covered by the modes of *rajas* and *tamas*. Spiritual development is a process of uncovering our qualities and fully manifesting them in our lives.

For years Donna struggled with her weight. "I had approached weight loss from a place of need," she said. She was constantly dissatisfied and distressed. To be satisfied she needed to have a thinner body. Then she could wear the clothes she wanted, and she'd feel happy. Donna shifted her paradigm and way of thinking. "I am a satisfied person, even if I never lose a pound." Donna's relationship with eating transformed, reflecting her change in consciousness. She became a conscious eater instead of an emotional eater, resulting in a different body shape. Donna continues, "There is no longer this battle going on, this huge war inside me. After I have my meal I'm not telling myself, 'You can't have more; you can't have a snack.' I'm saying, 'I'm fine. I'm satisfied.' From that platform I can choose. It feels a lot more peaceful." By connecting with her satisfied and peaceful being, Donna's *doing* and *having* with respect to eating, weight and health, were naturally transformed.

Certainly a fulfilled life includes having comforts and enjoyable things, and doing things that give us pleasure. Yet without being rooted in a life of meaning founded in and emanating from our spiritual being, possessions and activity are hollow, devoid of significance, like a string of zeros. Living from the inside outwards, from our spiritual core, is the "I" that gives value to the line of zeros.

To the degree that we are conditioned to identify ourselves materially and to live by paradigms such as Have-Do-Be, it requires effort to live from our spiritual core. At first this effort may feel like going against our grain. Be-Do-Have is not pretension. It is authentic connection with our essential quality, a way of being requiring conscious cultivation. Read further and discover an approach to living and relating based on transformative communication that steadily brings us towards our being.

PART TWO

Transformative
Communication:
Creating Sacred Space

Creating Sacred Space

Vasudeva listened with great attention; he heard all about [Siddhartha's] origin and childhood, about his studies, his seekings, his pleasures and needs. It was one of the ferryman's greatest virtues that, like few people, he knew how to listen. Without his saying a word, the speaker felt that Vasudeva took in every word, quietly, expectantly, that he missed nothing. He did not await anything with impatience and gave neither praise nor blame—he only listened. Siddhartha felt how wonderful it was to have such a listener who could be absorbed in another person's life, his strivings, his sorrows... 'I thank you,' said Siddhartha...'I thank you, Vasudeva, for listening so well. There are few people who know how to listen and I have not met anybody who can do so like you. I will learn from you in this respect.'

— Herman Hesse, *Siddhartha*

To be understood is a basic human desire. To know how to effectively listen and convey understanding is a key element in expressing love and care. Illuminating this principle, philosopher Paul Tillich once remarked that the first duty of love is to listen. Listening becomes especially important when we realize that as people we come together in community. A characteristic of genuine community is that conflicts and tensions are addressed, or communicated, in ways that enhance closeness and mutual understanding. According to psychologist Rollo May, "Communication leads to community, that is, to understanding, intimacy and mutual valuing." In this chapter we will examine communication principles and strategies that facilitate deeper connection on a spiritual level. These principles and techniques are effective for anyone interested in high-level interpersonal living.

MORE THAN WORDS

"When all other means of communication fail, try words."

Studies have shown that in expressing our feelings and attitudes, only about 7 percent of what we communicate is conveyed through words. About 38 percent of communication is paralinguistic, referring to certain qualities of our voice such as tone, emphasis, volume, inflection and pitch. Think about the vastly different paralinguistic behavior of saying "How are you doing?" as a social formality, compared with "How are you doing?" expressed to a person who is dear to us, whom we have not seen for many years.

Research has indicated that about 55 percent of communication regarding feelings and attitudes is nonverbal, meaning not related to our voice in any way. There have been studies with college students and their teachers in which the students knew they were part of the experiment and the professors were unaware they were being studied. During a lecture the students were instructed to exhibit classic elements of what is known as *attending behavior*. These include sitting squarely, in open-body position, leaning forward slightly and making comfortable eye contact. The result was that the professors would speak spontaneously, make eye contact and be animated in their motions. At a certain cue the students would switch to poor nonverbal attending behavior. The teachers' demeanor changed, becoming stiff. They began speaking in a monotone, looking down and reading from their notes. Although we may not be conscious of it, our nonverbal behavior affects others in a profound way.

The term *psychotherapy* derives from two Greek words: *psyche*, indicating the self or soul; and *therapeia*, meaning to attend to. To be a therapeutic influence for someone entails attending with our entire being, including our consciousness, words, tone, body language, and facial expressions. The physical aspects of proper attending behavior can be summed up as SOLE.

S = Sitting squarely

O = Open-body position

L = Leaning forward slightly

E = Eye contact

If we want to attend to someone, essentially we want to convey sincere interest, respect and caring, so that the person feels valued. Elements of SOLE are helpful in communicating this. Of course, in practical application we should consider circumstances such as culture. Eye contact between genders, or a particular amount of body space, may mean different things across different cultures. Or perhaps we may be speaking on the phone, or in a car, where constituents of standard good attending are not practical. However, when it is practically appropriate, applying SOLE will usually enhance mutual trust in communication.

WEG

Researchers have conducted a multitude of studies on the effects of the many types of therapies to determine which approaches are most effective in helping someone feel better and solve problems. These studies have indicated that outcomes are not primarily correlated with the type of counseling being practiced. What do correlate highly with positive outcomes are the qualities of the counselor. The essential qualities of an effective helper are *warmth, empathy* and *genuineness* (WEG). That is to say, regardless of the theoretical orientation of the counselor or school of techniques used, the extent to which the practitioners possessed warmth, empathy and genuineness directly corresponded with successful results. Warmth, empathy and genuineness are inherent qualities of the self. Thus effective helping is not dependent on university degrees or experience in the mental health professions. (In fact, such training can even be a barrier. In one study only about 13 percent of mental health professionals responded with empathy to a depressed client.)

Essential Qualities of an Effective Helper

W = Warmth
E = Empathy
G = Genuineness

It is important to note that true warmth is not a sentimental emotive expression. It is sincere understanding and caring. We do not want to use warmth to cover for lack of competence in communication skills. Natural warmth inspires trust. With empathy we understand the other person's perspective. This does not mean that we necessarily agree with that perspective; we can leave our frame of reference without abandoning it.

Genuineness means that we are authentic and spontaneous. While acknowledging that we may play various roles in life, we do not hide behind those roles. For example, though a person might recognize that he is the manager, child, youngest or senior member of a group, counselor or parent in a relationship, he does not allow these roles to become an obstacle to genuine human interaction.

ROADBLOCKS TO EFFECTIVE COMMUNICATION

Imagine that you are in your workplace, about to enthusiastically share some ideas at a staff meeting. Your supervisor, however, repeatedly shuts you down every time you want to express yourself. Afterwards you approach a colleague and say, "Can you believe how he ran that meeting? He didn't care what anyone had to say. And the way he treated me? I'm quitting this place!"

Below are several possible responses from your friend. After reading each statement, notice your gut reaction to it.

1. "You should sit down and talk with him. The two of you really need to clear things up, and I think you ought to initiate a conversation."

2. "With that attitude you'll be fired before you can quit, and let me tell you, you won't find it easy to get a new job."

3. "Just because you had a rough time at this one meeting is no reason to leave the company."

4. "I know that you are a resilient and tolerant person. You are one of the best employees in the office."

5. "Oh, don't worry, it will be okay."

6. "Life is like that, and you really need to accept it. Each of us takes it on the chin once in a while."

7. "It sounds to me like you have authority issues, probably stemming from unresolved anger toward your father."

8. "Hey, remember that restaurant we both really liked last week? Let's go there for lunch."

9. "Well, you have been lagging in producing those reports, so I don't think you are in a position to point your finger

at anyone. And also, you need to learn to speak up for yourself. You are not assertive enough."

10. "You're such a complainer."

The above attempts to "help" represent some fairly typical ways in which people respond when faced with a situation that is emotionally charged for the person addressing them. The following list describes the type of communication presented in each of the above statements:

1. advice; 2. warning; 3. logical argument; 4. praise; 5. reassurance; 6. philosophizing; 7. psychoanalyzing; 8. diverting; 9. criticizing; 10. name-calling.

Speaking for myself, none of the above responses would inspire me to express more to this person. If I am criticized or labeled I don't feel appreciated as a person. If advised, ordered, warned or analyzed, I feel like some sort of object, being manipulated to fulfill the agenda of someone else. Even if it is "good" advice, I won't necessarily feel heard and respected. Arguing or claiming that I shouldn't be feeling or experiencing what I am feeling is frustrating and even insulting. Even "positive" responses, such as praise or reassurance, seem patronizing to me.

The above types of response are potential roadblocks to effective communication. This is only a partial list. Other possible roadblocks include attack, defense, denial, sympathy, labeling, preaching, threat, and ordering. It is important to note that these responses do not always block communication. Each of these types of responses has its place in healthy communication. There is a time to give advice, a time to warn, to praise, and to criticize. As an initial response to someone in an emotionally charged state, however, these responses can often be experienced as interfering with the flow of expression. What we actually need to do is learn how to effectively use each type of response at the right time, making careful use of each one, just as a skilled carpenter would with each tool in his toolbox.

Roadblock responses tend to be about ourselves, rather than focused on the person who is expressing him or herself. We can also consider roadblocks within the framework of the three *gunas*, as described in the Be-Do-Have section. For example, a roadblock may be about my need, derived from the mode of *rajas*, to fix problems by giving solutions or offering advice, or my need, rooted in *tamas*, to avoid painful issues by changing the topic. Or they could relate to my desire for people to like me, through giving reassurance or praise, or my need to feel superior, by criticizing or categorizing.

Sattvic communication involves understanding things rightly as preliminary to response. In *sattvic* listening we genuinely focus on the other person. In this mode of illuminated, compassionate non-attachment, we are alert and attentive to the other person, without motive to coerce or manipulate. A roadblock does not necessarily mean that the responder lacks love or caring. Mastering *sattvic* communication skills offers us a powerful way to communicate our caring, concern and affection.

Potential Roadblocks to Effective Listening

· advising	· preaching	· analyzing
· judging	· teaching	· interpreting
· moralizing	· lecturing	· criticizing
· giving solutions	· ordering	· name-calling
· warning	· directing	· labeling
· threatening	· scolding	· sympathizing
· interrogating	· diverting	· reassuring
· probing	· distracting	· praising

EMPATHY AND A CULTURE OF TRUST

Consider once more the workplace scenario described above.

"Can you believe how he ran that meeting? He didn't care what anyone had to say. And the way he treated me? I'm quitting this place!"

Envision your response to the following comment: "You felt really insulted because of how he treated you during the meeting. I hear your anger toward the supervisor. You are so frustrated that you want to leave this place."

When someone really listens to me, deeply understands me and acknowledges the pain I am experiencing, I begin to feel less upset and more capable of handling my emotions and difficulties. Feeling cared about, I am moved to share more. Caring is reflected in listening, and an empathic response is an effective strategy to show that we have listened. Reflective, empathic responses build trust. If you reflect to me what I have said and the feeling behind the words, it is a sign that you truly care about me and what I have to say. This type of response is called *reflective listening*, or *mirroring*. In addition to creating a trusting environment, an empathic response enables me to reflect on myself. Just as I can see myself better by looking in a mirror, I can also see into my thoughts, emotions and experiences better if someone else takes the role of the mirror.

For example, in response to the above reflective comment, I might think to myself, "I am upset with him, though it's not that I really want to quit the job. There are many things I appreciate about this office—even about this new boss. I think I will talk to him. Maybe he is upset that I haven't turned in those reports. I may apologize about that, though I will let him know that I didn't appreciate how he spoke to me during the meeting."

Note that empathy is not sympathy. Sympathy can imply a sense of pity, such as is expressed in "I feel so bad for you." This does not convey an understanding of what the other person is saying, whereas a statement such as "I hear that you are feeling humiliated because she made a joke at your expense in a public forum" is an empathetic reflection that shows comprehension of content and affect.

Also, we can recognize that the statement "I understand" in itself is not a reflective statement. It is a declaration of knowledge. A statement such as "I understand that you are feeling unfulfilled because you know you can be more productive" is a reflective statement conveying empathy, because I have expressed not just that I understand, but what I understand to be the emotion and content of what the person is sharing. Of course, this does not mean that it is wrong to respond, "I understand." Accompanied with appropriate nonverbal behavior and caring intention, such a response can communicate empathy.

It is said that people don't care what we know until they know that we care. Demonstration of empathy is a wonderful way to show that we care. Empathic listening in itself creates a quality of human connection that is satisfying for the soul. And it produces an environment conducive for sharing whatever valuable knowledge we may have. In the field of social work there is a saying: "Start where the client is at." By meeting people where they are, we build trust, stimulate self-exploration, and clarify our perceptions.

Each scenario below includes roadblock replies and an empathic response. The roadblocks to effective communication are presented in terms of the roles we take in response to someone expressing himself or herself, roles such as *detective*, *magician*, or *florist*. For this imagery we gratefully acknowledge George Gazda et. al. and their book *Human Relations Development: A Manual for Educators*. As you read the situations below, think of instances when someone responded to you or you responded to someone else in these or similar ways that were not helpful. Recollect your experience at the time. Also, compare these reactions with your internal response to the *sattvic*, empathic reply.

Scenario 1

Student to teacher: "Every time in PE class I'm picked last. I don't think I'm such a terrible player, but honestly, it's starting to really affect me."

1. *Detective:* Who did this? What happened? Exactly how often has this happened? What? Where? When? Let's get all the details of the case!"

The Detective focuses on facts at the expense of appropriate attention to feelings. He controls the flow of conversation using the roadblock of probing, or interrogating, which can cause the speaker to feel defensive.

2. *Magician:* "Hey, the season is practically over, so it doesn't really make much of a difference anyway."

The Magician attempts to make the problem disappear by convincing the speaker that actually there is no difficulty. This illusion is temporary. Such false reassurance does not respect the validity of the speaker's perception and experience.

3. *Foreman:* "See these papers over here. I need them distributed before the next class starts. You think you could help me with this?"

Through the roadblock of diversion the Foreman minimizes and invalidates the speaker's expression. Effective communicators convey awareness of the depth, seriousness and intensity given by the speaker to any particular challenge.

4. *Hangman:* "Well I remember last year when you kept losing your temper whenever you played basketball. So what do you expect? Of course no one wants you on their team! You're getting just what you deserve."

The Hangman shows the person that he is guilty, that his prior behavior warrants the suffering and punishment. Such a perspective may be accurate, though the judgmental, critical comments of the Hangman are seldom helpful, because the speaker, at this juncture of the interaction, is unable to accept and utilize them. *Empathic responses:* "It must hurt to feel rejected when teams are chosen." Or, "I can imagine that it's really embarrassing for you to be the last one selected each time."

Scenario 2

Worker to colleague: "The head of the department just comes in with all these 'suggestions' about how to do things. It's completely impractical, and if we don't do it, he gets so upset."

1. *Forecaster:* "You better follow those suggestions. If you don't, then you'll really have something to worry about."

The Forecaster predicts what will happen. Declaring the forecast, this augur waits and watches for his predictions to materialize.

2. *Sign Painter:* "You're such a faultfinder! You're never satisfied and never will be, just like all the other disgruntled employees."

The Sign Painter's mentality is that a problem will be solved by giving it a name. Though classification systems have their value, ill-timed labeling and categorizing divests the speaker and the situation from their personal quality and unique character.

3. *Drill Sergeant:* "You should apply his ideas to your job. Think of it that way and you'll be fine."

Drill Sergeants give orders and expect them to be followed. They know what you should do, and are so convinced of their position that there isn't even a need to provide explanations of their dictates, and surely it is a waste of time to hear the speaker's feelings.

Empathic response: "It sounds like you're exasperated and irritated by the suggestions of the department head, which you think are pretty useless."

Scenario 3

Committee member to committee director: "You want me to lead the discussion at the next meeting. I'm just not able to do that. Please ask someone else. Every other member of the committee would do a better job than me."

1. *Dispenser of Wisdom:* "You'll never know what you're capable of unless you try. Even if you don't succeed, remember that failure is the pillar of success."

Dispensers of Wisdom bestow platitudes and catch-phrases as though they had privileged understanding of the wisdom of humankind. Their maxims, though, are impersonal, stereotyped, and generally don't adequately apply to any particular situation with potency or precision.

2. *Historian:* "I can definitely relate. I know what you're talking about. I remember one time when I was new at this agency...no, maybe it was the company where I used to work...anyway, I was asked to make a presentation about quarterly goals. I think that was the topic. So, I was so afraid of doing this and didn't want to, and so I spoke to the manager and she said..."

Historians excavate dreary old stories about themselves, and relate them in a way unlikely to be empathic, valuable or entertaining, at least at this early stage of the conversation.

Empathic response: "You seem frightened to assume this responsibility of leading the discussion. It seems to you to be more than you can manage."

Scenario 4

Parent to teacher: "Lydia's grades are still the same, even though we spent so much time with her. Last week you told us that if we worked with her then her grades would improve."

> *Florist:* "Oh, I'm sure that you're doing great with Lydia. I can tell by her attitude at school that you care so much about her! Whenever Lydia speaks about you she says the nicest things. You are providing a good home for her, that's for certain. Sometimes these things take time to work themselves out. And Lydia is trying harder. I'm sure it will be okay."

Uncomfortable to address anything with a scent of unpleasantness, Florists praise and reassure to keep real and substantial issues at a distance. Instead of facing conflict and tension, the Florist conceals them with bouquets of cheeriness.

Empathic response: "You're discouraged because although you're giving extra time, Lydia's grades have not improved."

Note that showing understanding is not just a matter of finding words to mechanically describe the person's emotion and content. It also includes matching the person's energy. When a friend is feeling sad and down, a reflective statement from my side in an excited voice won't yield understanding, although what I said was accurate. Empathy is more likely to be conveyed if our words are accompanied by an energy that matches the feeling of the situation. A discordant mentality, even if accompanied by correct reflective statements, can be a roadblock to effective communication. In this regard it is important to recognize that reflective listening is a tool that conveys the essence of empathy. Just because I make an accurate reflective statement does not necessarily mean that I am being empathetic. Conversely, it is possible to convey empathy while using a mode of communication that is on the "potential roadblock" list, although here we are focusing on techniques such as mirroring and effective attending to communicate empathy.

To experience the benefit of empathic dialogue, engage in it with some of the people in your life. Fully enter the world of the other person for at least fifteen minutes, using empathic listening to display understanding. Maintain comfortable eye contact and open-body position during the dialogue. Avoid roadblocks to communication. Simply be a mirror for the other person and notice your experience in attentively reflecting emotion and content. You can also switch roles, having the other person enter your world and mirror for you. To gain a real feel for the effect of empathic dialogue, the speaker should preferably talk about some issue that has an emotional charge for him or her. If you would like to increase the challenge, speak about an issue with emotional substance that is a source of tension between you and the other person. This process requires an ability to listen, and a commitment to understand.

By practicing dialogue in this format our communication becomes *dialogical* in spirit, even if we don't adhere to a framework of structured dialogue. In genuine dialogue I allow others to complete their communication, accepting their experience as real and valid for them. In listening I am not focusing on my next point. A dialogue is not a debate. We are actually listening to each other, not merely taking turns in *not listening*. Especially when discussing highly charged subjects, or when it is apparent that communication has broken down, utilizing structure for empathic conversation may be particularly valuable. Apply this in your life and notice a decrease in reactivity, increased emotional safety and deeper connection.

Creating sacred space between us entails commitment to genuine dialogue. Dialogue means that I listen with the intent to understand, rather than to counter or defeat. In a conscious dialogue, my intention in expression and hearing is not to manipulate, invalidate or prove that I am right. With true dialogue we create a sanctified environment, unadulterated by barriers to healthy communication. It is an enlightening experience. Educator Robert Hutchins comments, "Education is a kind of continuing dialogue, and a dialogue assumes different points of view." Approaching relationships with an attitude of discovery and deep listening means that diverse viewpoints enrich relations, rather than divide them.

To effectively live the principles and communication strategies described here requires that our consciousness rests in the mode of *sattva*—being able to observe while suspending judgment and being compassionate toward another being. Such compassion is the essence of empathy, and a fundamental quality of a spiritual life. There is a Vedic aphorism, *atmavat sarva-bhutesu*, which describes the essence of spiritual compassion as "feeling the happiness and distress of others as one's own."

Empathy connects us with others, emerges from and is cultivated through self-realization. Renowned management consultants Jagdish Sheth and Andrew Sobel write: "It is widely accepted that self-awareness and the ability to regulate your own emotions are fundamental prerequisites to the practice of empathy... If you can't tune into your own emotions, it's going to be a stretch trying to discern those of others. And if you are overcome by your own feelings, you'll never have the mental bandwidth to listen properly." Empathy requires a genuine interest in others, and a sincere desire to expand our perspectives and learning.

Effective in All Life Dimensions

There is a distinction between *thought empathy* and *feeling empathy*, both of which are important in connecting with people and their experience. Research has found that women are slightly more empathic than men with regards to feeling empathy, grasping the emotion behind the words. With reference to thought empathy—apprehending the thoughts behind words—studies have indicated no significant gender difference. An interesting aspect of this research is that after training in empathy, gender differences for both emotion empathy and thought empathy disappear. This indicates that men are not inherently less empathic than women. The lower degree of feeling empathy in men may be primarily determined by culture, meaning that showing empathy does not correspond with the image that a man wants to project, and thus men are less motivated to be empathetic. This cultural facet may be changing though, as there is increasing evidence—some of which is cited below—that effectiveness in traditionally male-oriented occupations is associated with high empathy.

Across many fields of endeavor, including those where we might not imagine that listening and relationship skills are preeminent, empathy is understood to be an essential quality for success. In his book *Emotional Intelligence*, Daniel Goleman quotes the head of a Swiss bank: "My job is something like a family priest or doctor. You can't be in private banking without using your emotional intelligence, especially empathy. You have to sense what your client hopes for, fears—even if he can't express it in words." Empathy is the most important quality in the assessment of applicants to the Harvard Business School's graduate program, and the top five attributes are all "soft" qualities, such as being a team player and being able to effectively coach people and understand their perspective.

Research has shown that in a multitude of professions, including police work, financial consulting, and sales, higher empathy correlates positively with better performance, results and satisfaction. A study at a large polyester fiber plant demonstrated that empathy was the quality that most differentiated the most productive teams of workers from others. In the field of medicine, greater empathy correlates positively with more accurate diagnoses, higher patient satisfaction and other desirable outcomes. In a study comparing physicians who were sued for malpractice with physicians who weren't, the quality that most distinguished the group that did not get sued was empathy. The doctors who were not litigated against were not necessarily more skilled. They were more empathetic, which meant that if an apparent mistake did occur patients were less likely to file suit.

Empathy does not mean sentimentally acceding to the demands of others. Knowing how the other person feels and being able to show it does not mean agreeing with them. I can understand and be open to another perspective, while standing for my own viewpoint. This quality of empathy and the skill to express it underlies effectiveness across practically all life dimensions. Below we further explore benefits of manifesting empathy.

Foster Self-Exploration

Consider the following conversation from a coaching session with a young adult, who thought he had clearly decided to move out of his parent's home. After some deliberation, he expressed misgivings. While the mirroring in these conversations may seem excessive at times, the purpose of these real life examples is to emphasize the compelling effects of empathic listening.

Client: I have doubts about leaving my parents' home.

Coach: Though a few days ago you determined that you will move out of the home of your parents, upon reflection you are unsure whether that is actually the best move for you.

Client: Yeah. My situation here is convenient, and there will be so many things to arrange if I'm on my own.

Coach: While you are attracted to having more autonomy and independence, you are also appreciating the comfort and convenience of your present situation. You are reluctant to move. You are really uncertain whether this is the right time.

Client: That's true. Then again, I had this same conversation with myself a year ago. I know there will be challenges, and at some point I need to face them. It may as well be now. I'm really feeling stuck here at home.

Looking into the mirror of the coach's responses, the client reflects and sees more deeply into himself. While clarifying the advantages and consequences of remaining where he is, he also revisits the possibility of moving, along with the challenges this brings. The coach continues to empathize, reflecting the content and emotion of the client's expression.

Coach: You realize that for at least a year you've considered moving out. The same considerations stopping you then are stopping you now. Looking at this, you're feeling stuck and not fully expressed in your life.

Client: Yeah, it's definitely time to move out. I know I've made the right decision.

Coach: You sound clear that it is time for you to move on, out on your own.

The coach reflects the clarity of thought and action declared by the client. Empathic understanding has helped this person to see himself and get clear about what he wants. Note that the coach did not advise or attempt to solve the problem for the client. The coach listened and demonstrated his listening through mirroring, stimulating the client to explore the matter further.

Compare the above with the following dialogue.

Client: I have doubts about leaving my parent's home.

Coach: Don't be ridiculous. You have already decided it's time to leave the nest. Now it's time to follow through.

Client: I'm not sure if I'm ready.

Coach: There's no time like the present.

Client: Actually, I don't think I am ready. Maybe next year.

In this example, contesting the doubts with roadblocks——for example platitudes, ordering and minimization—leads to resistance. The coach did not facilitate the speaker in honestly exploring and clarifying his feelings. Whereas in the first scenario the coach's understanding drained defensiveness and energized the client toward productive realization, in the second dialogue a lack of understanding intensified the opposition.

Here is another case study. With the help of a coach, Dana is exploring the nature of her participation in a personal development group in which she is the youngest member.

Dana: I know that I'm getting value from this group, and I will complete the program. It's just that I am a lot younger than all the other members, and I do wonder if it would be better for me to do the program with peers.

Coach: Though you know you are benefiting from the group experience, you have some dissatisfaction, some doubt, about whether this is the best group for you. You think it may be more valuable for you to do this program with people of similar age.

Dana: Yeah, that's right. Though when you say it like that, I realize that I don't really have friends my age. I mean, there are people I party with, and have fun; but no one who I share deeply with.

The coach simply mirrors in his own words what Dana shares with him. In this safe interpersonal environment, Dana acknowledges the truth of what she has expressed, and this moves her to the more profound issue of friendship.

Coach: It seems that this topic has connected you with the issue of friendship in your life. You seem to be feeling a lack of rewarding connections with persons around your age.

Dana: Yes. With the group members, and with some others who are a lot older than me, I have meaningful conversations. But not with the friends that I hang out with just to have a good time.

Coach: Your dissatisfaction seems to be about a lack of rewarding, meaningful connection with friends who are your age.

Dana: I wish I could create with them the sort of relations I have with the group members. But they're not that type. I really don't think it's their age. It's their personalities, which are compatible with me for partying, but not for something more significant.

The coach empathically stays with Dana, as she sharpens the distinctions of her comprehension, discerning the differences in effects of the factors of age and personality.

Coach: It sounds like you're realizing that the essential factor here isn't age, but rather compatibility of personalities.

Dana: Yes, with the group members I'm fulfilled, and it's not about their age. I connect with their commitment to growth. And with my friends, I mostly feel empty.

Through the agency of the coach's empathic listening, Dana progresses from the topic of her participation in the group to the core issue of not being fulfilled in her peer friendships. Note that reflection of feeling and content is the only strategy that the coach uses to assist Dana in achieving her insights.

Diffusing Hostility

In my communication seminars I am often asked about diffusing hostility. An empathic response is the most powerful means for diffusing aggressiveness. In the mid-nineties I worked as a children and family counselor for the State of Florida Department of Foster Care. On one occasion an enraged father stormed into my office. "How could you tell the judge to keep my kid in foster care!?" Many responses were available to me. I could have yelled back, perhaps referring to his continued substance abuse or his irresponsibility in fulfilling his performance agreement. This would have likely escalated his fury. Or I could have calmly explained to him what he could do to get his child returned, which was the outcome that both of us desired. I began with empathy, matching his intensity. "I know you are furious with me. You're upset that I recommended to the judge to keep your child in foster care for another three months." He continued his tirade, and I continued my attempts at showing my understanding of what he expressed. I would not say that at any point in this conversation did this person develop a liking for me. However, after a few minutes he did sense that I was not his enemy, and that I cared about him and his son. His anger diffused through empathic listening and we were able to have a civilized and productive dialogue, during which I did share with him information about what he could do to accelerate the process of his child's return. Once he knew that I cared, he began to care what I knew.

My wife and I once attended a lecture on Vedic spirituality, the theme of which was transferring consciousness from *ahankara* to *atman*. Ahankara refers to our false, materially based identifications, such as "I am white," "I am fifty-two years old," or "I am Peruvian." Atman refers to identification with our true spiritual identity. On the ride home my wife shared an exchange she had had that day with a doctor, in her capacity as a nurse who inserts intravenous lines. The doctor had ordered a line inserted in a patient although Miriam, noticing various signs and symptoms indicating that it would not be medically advisable to do so, decided not to.

Doctor: I ordered the line put in!

Miriam: I see you're very upset because I didn't put in the line.

Doctor: Who the hell do you think you are!? I gave my orders and it's not done!

Miriam: I know you're really angry with me because I didn't follow your orders about this.

Doctor: Yeah, that's right. I've got so much to do and I wrote the instructions. I made it clear!

Miriam: I know you're very pressured, under so much strain, and it's so annoying for you that I didn't put in the line. It's extra anxiety—just what you didn't need today.

Doctor: That's right. How come you didn't put in the line?

Miriam explained her reasons and they engaged in calm, rational dialogue about the best course of action for the patient. After describing this interaction to me, Miriam said of the doctor, "He went from *ahankara* to *atman*."

A particularly challenging occasion for reflective listening arises when acrimony is directed toward us by persons with whom we are in a close relationship. A student once wrote the following to me: "One area that I find is very relevant for workshop participants …is the difficulty of doing empathic listening when a spouse or person very close to us is saying something that we totally disagree with. I once made great sacrifices for my wife and then she told me she didn't like what I did and her reasons were totally uninformed. At that point I couldn't imagine doing empathic listening. I was so upset I just screamed. It's one of the most needed and most challenging times to do empathic listening."

I replied: "I hear your challenge and frustration. It is relatively easy to empathize and reflect when the hostility, anger and resentment are directed toward some third party. When it's directed toward us it is especially challenging to be *sattvic*, non-reactive, empathic and compassionate. It is particularly difficult in those instances, and also especially important. When we are able to notice our anger, pain or fear without giving our power to them, and to instead sincerely endeavor to understand the other person, before expressing what we want to say, we create the climate in these close and intimate relationships that we truly desire."

At the start of the second day of a five-day seminar, a woman who was attending shared her experience from the previous night, after the first day of the seminar when we had covered empathic listening. "My son was in the bath and wanted to play with a particular bottle of liquid soap. I knew this soap would hurt his eyes and wouldn't allow it. In the past this sort of scene would lead to an escalation of anger, affecting us, and the household, for at least a full day if not longer. 'No, you can't have it!' 'I want it!' 'I said no! Put it down!' Instead I thought I'll use the skills we learned that day in the workshop. 'You're really angry at mommy for not letting you play with that soap!' 'Yes, I want it!' 'I know you really wish you could have that bottle, and you're mad at me because I won't let you.' 'That's right. I am.' I couldn't believe it. After about a minute the episode was over. His anger was gone, and we enjoyed each other's company."

Studies in labor-management discussions demonstrate that it takes half the time to achieve conflict resolution when all parties agree to accurately repeat what the previous speaker has said before responding. To do this requires *sattvic* consciousness, where we are attentive and sufficiently patient to mirror the other person's statement, before saying our piece. Especially when we are in conflict with the other party, it requires substantial non-attachment to utilize reflective empathy and avoid roadblocks. Frequently in workshops I hear, "But David, using these techniques takes much longer." My response is, "Yes, maybe it does. In the short run." *Sattvic* communication may take longer up front. However, in the long run it avoids the anxieties and problems created by roadblock-filled *tamasic* and *rajasic* communication. For instance, we might spend more time in mirroring and empathic listening so that we understand an employee; his satisfaction, though, results in a more pleasant work environment where people want to stay. This in turn is likely to lead to higher efficiency and an increase in productivity.

Inspiration to Action

In the safe and trusting environment created through empathic listening, we are inspired to explore deeply, which often leads to problem-resolution. We may have a great idea how to help someone resolve a challenge, or at least think we do. Reflective listening in *sattva guna* is based on the assumption that each of us possesses the capacity to handle his or her life with excellence. The necessary qualities and knowledge are within us. Usually it is more powerful to facilitate a person in generating his own solution rather than simply presenting him ours. If I arrive at an idea, I am more likely to commit to it and apply it in my life if it has not been provided by someone else. And often we find that our "great ideas" for someone else aren't actually so great. Sometimes, because we did not carefully listen, our solutions are based on mistaken assumptions.

In the following case scenario Susan, supported by the reflections of the coach, augments her self-realization and concretizes an action plan.

Susan: I don't want to encourage him. I think he may fall in love with me. Actually, he said that he is worried about this.

Coach: You're afraid to give him encouragement. He expressed that he is worried about falling in love with you, and this scares you.

Susan: Yes. At the same time I like him. I don't want to be unkind. I don't know what to do.

Responding to the coach's reflection of content and feeling, Susan broadens her exploration of the matter.

Coach: You want to be nice to him. You don't want to be mean. You're afraid to hurt his feelings. And also you're fearful to attract him to fall in love. This is a conflict inside you.

Susan: Yes. I don't know how to be with him. Before I was very natural.

Coach: You had a good friendship, and now you're uncertain how to be with this person. You don't want to falsely encourage him, and you don't want to lose him from your life.

Susan: From my side also, I am afraid...to fall in love. But I value our friendship, and don't want to lose that.

Like peeling the layers of an onion, Susan's exploration, facilitated by the *active listening* of the coach, leads her to see beneath the surface of what she initially presented, and to focus on her fears and desires related to a romantic relationship.

Coach: You're attracted to him, and you're open to the possibility of a romantic relationship developing. Also, you are worried about losing your friendship with him.

Susan: And this has happened before. In my confusion I just pushed these men friends away. I would be mean.

Susan recognizes a pattern in her behavior, across time and relationships.

Coach: Your habit from the past is that you'd be unkind, and create a situation where they'd leave.

Susan: Yes, but I know I don't have to be like that.

Through this empathic dialogue, Susan opens to new possibilities about how she can act in relationships. She does not need to be unkind or harsh to others as a reaction to her own confusion and fear.

Coach: I hear that you really don't want to put up a wall that will prevent you from whatever relationship could develop, and you know you don't have to.

Susan: It's a fear of myself, not trusting myself. Because I don't trust myself, I don't assert myself, and play games and put up walls. I don't want to cause pain.

Coach: You're scared to really stand for what's true for you.

Susan: Yes. And it's important for me to speak with him. I have been so withheld with him, and I do want to directly address this.

Susan clarifies that she wants to directly express herself to her friend about their relationship. For Susan, a result of being heard and understood is that she finds the courage to be clear, to abandon former ineffective relationship habits and to cultivate healthier ways of communicating and relating.

Coach: Just like you're expressing yourself to me, you want to be able to do that with him, to talk with your friend about what's going on between you and him.

Susan: He has shown a lot of courage. He did his part in sharing vulnerably with me. Now it's time for me to do my part.

Coach: You want to reciprocate. He showed courage and you admire that, and now you want to be courageous with him. What's your plan for this?

Susan: I will talk with him, by next Monday. As soon as possible.

Susan moves from confusion to clarity, and from commitment to action, through this transformative dialogue. Now, for the sake of comparison, suppose the listener had initially responded in the following way:

Susan: I don't want to encourage him. I think he may fall in love with me. Actually, he said that he is worried about this.

Coach: Definitely you should speak with him. Share openly with him what's true for you.

Though such advice may sound sensible, when the listener begins by advising, the client misses the opportunity for self-exploration and for generating his or her own personal realizations.

Self-Correcting Process

George Bernard Shaw said, "The single biggest problem in communication is the illusion that it has taken place." Reflective listening is an effective means to dispel that illusion because it is a self-correcting process. Suppose I share with you that "I didn't get the job." Then you give me advice about how I can restore my self-esteem, carry on with determination in applying for other positions, warn me about the dire situation of my finances, tell me that I shouldn't be angry because everyone gets rejected sometimes, and so on. And I am sitting there thinking, "I'm glad I didn't get that job. It would have limited me so much. Already I have pursued possibilities with my flexible, independent schedule that have brought in significantly more income than that dead end job." Now suppose that instead of advising, warning and other road-blocks, you had begun with a *reflection*: "You must be angry, upset and discouraged that you didn't get the job." I would have corrected you, "I'm not angry or discouraged. I'm excited about the options that are open to me. Definitely it's a blessing that I didn't get that job." Though your reflection was inaccurate, I still received the message that you care about what I have to say, that I matter. And from the resulting dialogue you would have received clarification on what was true for me. Despite the imperfect attempt at mirroring, real communication would have taken place.

In the next dialogue, active listening moves Jackie to a realization of what she can gain through transformation of her self-view. She sees how she trains others not to feel comfortable with her, and recognizes her responsibility for her experience in relationships. Toward the end of the conversation is an exchange that illustrates the self-correcting nature of the process of empathic dialogue.

Jackie: With most people, even people close to me, like my sister, I'm not comfortable with myself. I don't know what to say, how to react.

Coach: You feel awkward with people, not secure with yourself. You'd like to be comfortable with yourself, to live with confidence.

Jackie: That would change a lot of things. I'm so scared of what people will think.

In response to the reflection of the coach, Jackie starts with "not comfortable" and proceeds to a core emotion of "scared."

Coach: You worry what people will think about you. It would make a real difference for you to be genuinely confident.

Jackie: It definitely would. In talking to you I am becoming aware of some things. Because I'm not confident, they aren't secure with me. I don't express myself because I'm so afraid, and then others don't trust me.

Coach: Your experience of yourself affects their experience of being with you. Because you are not sure of yourself, others don't trust you.

Jackie: That's right. My sister doesn't know what I'm thinking, where I'm standing about things, about her, so she has a sense of uncertainty, mistrust of me.

In this empathic dialogue, with the coach entering, understanding and reflecting her worldview, Jackie broadens her outlook and becomes conscious of how others react to her, and why.

Coach: If you change, they'll also change how they relate with you.

Jackie: As it is now, my relationships are fuzzy, because I don't clearly share myself.

Coach: You see that your relationships are unclear, because you are fuzzy in what you express.

Jackie: Exactly. It's unclear, because I'm not being clear. Actually I am changing. I know I am. I am beginning to relate in a new way, but I'm not accustomed to it.

Coach: You are becoming clearer in your expression of yourself. You're still uneasy, though, with this new way of relating to people.

Jackie: Not uneasy. I'd say confused. I like my new way of being. But I think, "What am I supposed to say now? What should I do?" People react to me differently and I don't know what to do with it. So I withdraw again.

Although the reflection of "uneasy" was not fully accurate, it gave the client an opportunity to refine the understanding of the coach. Thus, although the reflection was flawed, the result was an even deeper, more precise understanding for both speaker and listener. A symptom of the *sattvic* mode is enlightenment. We see that even if our attempts to utilize empathic listening are flawed, they result in expanded knowledge for everyone involved.

The following diagram depicts communication as a code sent by a sender and decoded by a receiver.

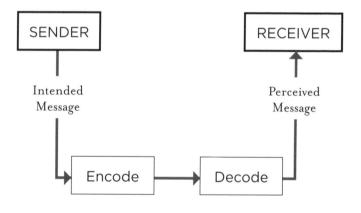

Miscommunication happens in the decoding process. Through reflective listening we check to see whether we have properly decoded the message. If we have, that's great. If not, we become aware of it.

SILENCE

"If A equals success, then the formula is A equals X plus Y and Z, with X being work, Y play, and Z keeping your mouth shut."

—Albert Einstein

In the novel *Momo*, Michael Ende creates the character of a young girl, who is a wonderful example of an empathic listener, and whose silent presence helps people connect with their inner truth. Momo receives a daily stream of visitors, eager to be close to her.

Was Momo so incredibly bright that she always gave good advice, or found the right words to console people in need of consolation...? No, she was no more capable of that than anyone else of her age...what Momo was better at than anyone else was listening. She listened in a way that made slow-witted people have flashes of inspiration. It wasn't that she actually said anything or asked questions that put such ideas into their heads. She simply sat there and listened with the utmost attention...fixing them with her big, dark eyes, and they suddenly became aware of ideas whose existence they had never suspected. Momo could listen in such a way that worried and indecisive people knew their own minds from one moment to the next, or shy people felt suddenly confident and at ease, or down-hearted people felt happy and hopeful. And if someone felt that his life had been an utter failure, and that he himself was only one among millions of wholly unimportant people who could be replaced as easily as broken windowpanes, he would go and pour out his heart to Momo. And, even as he spoke, he would come to realize...he was absolutely wrong: that there was only one person like himself in the whole world, and that, consequently, he mattered to the world in his own particular way. Such was Momo's talent for listening...Those who still think that listening isn't an art should see if they can do it half as well.

Silence itself is a potent listening tool, and can convey a grasp of another person's emotions. While silence should not be used to avoid intimate and meaningful conversation, neither is it helpful to avoid silence due to feelings of discomfort. Often we fill silence with empty talk, fearing the vulnerability of silent connection. An attentive, caring silence is sometimes a more powerful way to heal and connect than the most carefully chosen and well-intentioned words. Actual silence means that the mind is also still. Silence doesn't mean "empty." It is a gateway to, and manifestation of, spiritual presence. Vedic scholar Bhaktivedanta Swami wrote, "Silence means that one is always thinking of self-realization." It is said that God has given us two ears and one mouth, because we are meant to listen at least twice as much as to speak. The *Bhagavad Gita* describes true silence as a reflection of the divine within us. In empathic silence we are listening to what the other person is saying, not to what we are saying about what the other person is saying. That is, we are attuned to the person's words and the emotion and intention behind the words, not to our judgments, planned responses or comments towards the other person's self-expression. We are deeply listening, receiving another person with full presence, intense interest and an open heart. Such listening expands the spirits of both speaker and listener.

SERVICE THROUGH
EMPATHIC LISTENING

Another character from a novel, Josephus in Herman Hesse's *The Father Confessor*, was renowned as a great healer. In Josephus

> a gift slumbered, and with the passing years...it slowly came to flower. It was the gift of listening. Whenever a brother from one of the hermitages, or a child of the world harried and troubled of soul, came to Josephus and told him of his deeds, sufferings, temptations, and missteps...or spoke of his loss, pain or sorrow, Josephus knew how to listen to him, to open his ears and heart, to gather the man's sufferings and anxieties into himself and hold them, so that the penitent was sent away emptied and calmed...

> He regarded every man the same way, whether he accused God or himself, whether he magnified or minimized his sins and sufferings, whether he confessed a killing or merely an act of lewdness, whether he lamented an unfaithful sweetheart or the loss of his soul's salvation. It did not alarm Josephus when someone told of converse with demons...He did not lose patience when someone talked at great length while obviously concealing the main issue...All the complaints, confessions, charges, and qualms that were brought to him seemed to pour into his ears like water into the desert sands. He seemed to pass no judgment upon them and to feel neither pity nor contempt for the person confessing. Nevertheless, or perhaps for that very reason, whatever was confessed to him seemed not to be spoken into the void, but to be transformed, alleviated, and redeemed in the telling and being heard. Only rarely

did he reply with a warning or admonition, even more rarely did he give advice, let alone any order. Such did not seem to be his function, and his callers apparently sensed that it was not. His function was to arouse confidence and be receptive, to listen patiently and lovingly, helping the imperfectly formed confession to take shape, inviting all that was dammed up or encrusted within each soul to flow and pour out...

Josephus experienced severe struggles, and discovered his own healing in entering the world of others, serving them as an instrument in their healing. To serve another person—be it as a friend caring for a friend or a businessperson serving a customer—means understanding the needs, desires, thoughts and emotions of that person. This is empathy, a way of being that creates a culture of trust, supports self-realization and generates a climate of healing and healthy resolution. This is a key quality in life-enriching relationships that are based on honor and respect for each individual.

The essence of these techniques and principles—such as empathy, effective attending behavior and appropriate silence—is to view the world from the other person's perspective. Seeing the worldview of someone does not mean being in agreement with that view. We can be secure in our viewpoint while understanding another perspective. In fact, an internal sense of security naturally translates to an openness to other frames of reference. Below we consider open-ended questions, another important listening tool.

OPEN-ENDED QUESTIONS

"Computers are useless. They can only give you answers."

—Pablo Picasso

Open-ended questions are another valuable listening tool. Effectively utilized, they encourage the speaker to share more. A closed-ended question is one that invites a one-word answer. Some examples of closed-ended questions:

"How many years have you been at this job?"

"Were you happy in high school?"

"How many siblings do you have?"

An assumption behind closed-ended questions is that the questioner determines what is important. Open-ended questions assume that the person being questioned decides what is most essential. Examples of open-ended invitations include:

"What is your experience in this job?"

"I'd like to hear more about what high school was like for you."

"Could you speak more about your relationship with your brothers and sisters?"

"What is your confusion about?"

Closed-ended questions have their healthy place in communication, though usually the information sought with a closed-ended question comes automatically—along with much more—in response to an open-ended query. For example, once I had a new client who expressed that she wanted to have a child. Though I considered that knowing whether she was nineteen or forty-two might be helpful information, I didn't ask, "How old are you?" The conversation included open-ended questions such as, "What's happening in your relationship with your partner on this issue of children?" and, "What would having a child mean for you?" In the natural course of conversation, the client disclosed that she was twenty-nine years old, without my needing to make it my specific agenda to gather that piece of information.

Appropriately used, questions help people to talk about themselves and concretely define their challenges and situations in terms of specific experiences, behaviors and emotions. Suppose someone says, "My family life is a mess." With an open-ended question—such as "What is it about your family life that's not satisfying for you?"—we invite the speaker to describe his situation more tangibly. He might respond, "My job has me traveling so much, and I can barely pay the bills. And my children are constantly fighting. I don't know how to handle them." At that point it may be appropriate to follow this with empathy, showing understanding of affect and content. "I hear that so much travel is stressful for you, and you're experiencing a lot of financial strain. Also, you're frustrated with your children." This reflection could serve as a prompt for the speaker to further explore any one of the three areas. Though open-ended questions are a powerful listening tool because they show interest in the client's world, keep in mind that too many consecutive questions can be a roadblock, causing the person to feel interrogated. An effective question will elicit rich information, and often it is valuable to follow the question with a reflective response to ensure that we've grasped the information.

Concreteness is another important principle in effective communication. If we find conversations to be uninteresting, it may be a sign that we lack concreteness, instead talking with excessive generalities. Concreteness comes with clarity, excitement and the potential to augment understanding, growth and connection. For example if I say, "I just don't feel right," my statement is vague. Your discovery about me will be enriched if I express with concreteness that, "I was awake all night studying. I don't feel confident about the material, and I'm exhausted, and this test means everything about my future in the program." An open-ended question is often an excellent means to encourage concrete expression.

Clarity in expression greatly influences people's perception of us. Austrian statesman Metternich said, "Anything that is good in itself must be capable of being expressed clearly and precisely. The moment I come across words that are not very clear, I am left with the conclusion that they are either mistaken or deceitful." As a suggestion for practicing concreteness in your life, describe an experience in writing—first vaguely, and then concretely. (For example, "Today was a downer" is an imprecise expression of experience, whereas "I had a terrible headache during my entire work day" is a concrete statement.)

EXERCISES

There is a Chinese proverb that says, "I hear and I forget; I see and I remember; I do and I understand." In order that this book may make an auspicious and profound difference in your life, communication and relationships, I have provided practical exercises to integrate the principles and techniques discussed here. Above we spoke of a communication toolbox. Below are exercises to help you cultivate, integrate and sharpen these valuable tools. This will assist you in your self-development and in confidently asserting yourself.

Exercise 1

Below are scenarios with statements, each followed by four responses. For each response indicate whether it is an empathic response or not. If the response is a roadblock to effective communication, state what type of block it is, and consider how the speaker might feel in reaction to such a statement. (My responses are in Appendix B.)

Example: Woman in her early thirties to an employment counselor:

"I can do these jobs as well as...no, better than, most of these college graduates. I have so much life experience— valuable experience that gives me an edge in dealing with people. And I do read a lot. Mark Twain said, 'Don't let college interfere with your education.' I see so many people stunted in their actual progress by college. I really cringe when the first thing I'm asked is 'Highest degree earned?' Then I answer and I see they just shut me out after that."

A) Maybe if you got an associate's degree that would help in your job search. *[Advice]*

B) Hey, you know, yesterday evening I saw your husband and son at the little league game. They look great. *[Diverting. Distracting]*

C) You have learned so much on your own. You're really so smart. *[Praising. Not addressing the situation of the speaker.]*

D) You know that you are educated and capable of doing many of these jobs very effectively. You resent being labeled as "only a high-school graduate" and disqualified on the basis of that categorization. [Accurate empathy]

Scenario 1

Man in his twenties to a friend:

"I'm just trying to be sociable. But I seem to alienate every-one by being overly friendly. I even think the reason I got fired was related to that, though they didn't actually say it. And, well, it doesn't seem to work with women very well. I've been told my humor is over the edge. But I'm just being who I am, I think."

A) You sound sad and disappointed because many people find your interpersonal style to be annoying and irritat-ing. This is disturbing for you. As far as you're aware, you're just being natural.

B) You're projecting onto others what is true about yourself. You're being irresponsible, not seeing your own part in how others treat you.

C) Everyone has their quirks, and their strengths. You'll be okay.

D) Yeah, tone it down. Listen more than you speak. And stop being so insecure.

Scenario 2

Child, aged ten, to parent:

"I'm not cold. I don't want to wear a jacket."

A) It's almost freezing today. You're stupid not to wear a coat.

B) You're not feeling cold, and you don't want to wear a jacket.

C) Don't wear a jacket. Go ahead. You'll be the one who gets really sick.

D) We have to learn to take care of ourselves. I know you're only ten, but my job is to teach you how to be responsible. When you get older no one else is going to take care of you. So you should learn to do that for yourself now. And when you have children you'll know what I mean.

Scenario 3

Employee to colleague:

"This is the third time this week my supervisor saw me return from lunch more than half an hour late. I don't know what's going to happen now."

A) You're a good worker. You can always find another job.

B) You're scared because you think you might get fired.

C) Well, that's your fault. Why do you act like that anyway?

D) You reap what you sow. You wouldn't like it if you were the supervisor and an employee acted like this. Do unto others…

Exercise 2

A typical format for an empathic, reflective response is "You feel _____ because _____ "—with the first blank being a reflection of affect, and the second a reflection of content. Below are a few sample scenarios. In the first set of lines below the statement write a response that you believe would be a roadblock for the speaker. After that, write a reflective response, in the format described above, that you believe would convey empathy.

In life our reflective statements will naturally vary from the standard format, "You feel _____ because _____." According to your communication style, you may perhaps be more comfortable with "You seem....," "You sound...," "It appears that you are feeling...," or any one of numerous other possibilities. For the sake of practice and skill development, use the "You feel _____ because _____" framework for the statements below. My responses are in Appendix B.

1. I've been so depressed since I got the diagnosis. I don't even want to continue living anymore.

_____

_____

_____

_____

_____

_____

2. This is the second month in a row I didn't get even close to my sales goal. And I'm late with my reports. I can tell by the way the manager looks at me that I'm real close to being tossed out.

_____

_____

_____

_____

_____

_____

3. I was sure I flunked that test. And I got an 'A' minus. I can't believe it.

_____

_____

_____

_____

_____

4. My parents really want me to go directly to college. One group of friends wants me to travel with them for a year, and others are already working and earning money and recommended I do the same. I don't know what to do.

_____

_____

_____

_____

_____

5. I'm successful in my life, in so many areas. It's just that I know I can do more.

_____

_____

_____

_____

_____

It happens to all of us that at times we have something difficult to say, something that might be unpleasant for others to hear. How should we go about expressing ourselves? There are three basic ways to do so, which correspond to the three main modes of material nature, as discussed before. These three modes are *passivity, assertiveness and aggressiveness*. Corresponding qualities connected with each mode of expression are given below.

Passivity	Assertiveness	Aggressiveness
• scared	• bold	• abrasive
• insecure	• confident	• cocky
• nervous	• considerate	• harsh
• inhibited	• secure	• bully
• anxious	• empathetic	• arrogant
• self-deprecating	• straightforward	• insensitive
• weak	• honest	• loud
• fragile	• courageous	• obnoxious
• indecisive	• open	• selfish

It is obvious that assertiveness is the most desirable form of expression. Consider the following example. Say that Robert has agreed with his wife Lisa that he will be home from work at 6 p.m., and that he will call if he is late. How will she react when he comes home at midnight several nights in a row without calling her? In a passive mode, she may not say anything out of fear of disturbing the peace, whereas inside herself she may be building anger and mistrust. This is related to the mode of *tamas*, which is distinguished by fear and inactivity. In an aggressive mode she may scream and threaten Robert. This correlates with the mode of *rajas*, characterized by reactivity.

Neither of these modes is likely to create productive communication. If Lisa is passive, Robert may not even be aware that there is a problem, and may appreciate his wife for her tolerance and understanding. If she is aggressive, decent communication is likely to be hindered as well, and Robert may either withdraw or answer with hostility from his side. None of these exchanges—*fight* or *flight*—culminates in frank and satisfying discussion.

With passivity, Lisa's implicit message is: "You count. I don't." With aggressiveness it is: "I count. You don't." Assertiveness conveys, "You matter, as do I." In assertiveness we take a stand, make our voice heard, in a way that honors others. Assertiveness is simultaneously bold and empathic, courageous and considerate. This quality of assertiveness is inherent to our integrity as human beings. A life of integrity entails expressing what we are meant to express in an honest and gentle way. Lacking this, we live a life controlled by fear. Integrity also demands that in expressing ourselves we are respectful of others, and that in claiming our rights we also honor the rights of others. Assertiveness means that even if we are expressing a truth that may be difficult or painful for others to receive, we are not doing it in a hurtful way. It is possible to speak about that which is unpleasant without actually *being* unpleasant. Rather than attempting to do damage, we endeavor to understand and to be understood—from a place of compassion.

WIN

Through assertiveness we avoid roadblocks to clean communication in our expression. Being respectful and secure with assertive statements, we stay away from such roadblocks as name-calling, diverting and threatening. A strategy that may help us to cultivate assertive expression is WIN, an acronym standing for:

W = What happened

I = Inside feelings and thoughts

N = Needs and wants

In the *What happened* part we simply state the facts. We are not interpreting or analyzing them. In the example above this might sound like, "You agreed to be home by 6 p.m., and to call me if you were going to be late. Three days in the past two weeks you arrived home after midnight without calling me." In this statement Lisa isn't exclaiming, "You don't love me!" or, "You're a lousy husband." She is simply and accurately stating the facts.

The next part is *Inside feelings and thoughts*. In assertive expression these feelings and thoughts are delivered with "I" statements. "I" statements are a key feature of powerful, effective communication. Using "I" statements is a compelling way to be responsible for our communication. After carefully stating the facts, Lisa might then express, "I am hurt by this. I feel disrespected and angry with you." Notice the difference between "I" statements and "you" statements, such as "You are so irresponsible," or "You are the most insensitive person."

Illustrating the distinction between facts and reactions to facts, Marshall Rosenberg, founder of the Center for Nonviolent Communication, poetically expressed it thus:

> I can handle your telling me
>   what I did or didn't do
> And I can handle your interpretations
>   but please don't mix the two.
> If you want to confuse any issue,
>   I can tell you how to do it;

Mix together what I do
with how you react to it.
Tell me that you're disappointed
with the unfinished chores you see,
But calling me "irresponsible"
is no way to motivate me...

There is a significant difference between an "I" statement such as "I am angry that you came home so late," and a "you" statement such as "You made me angry." Though the distinction may seem subtle, there is an important difference in the message and effect. If I say, "You make me angry," where is the power for my anger? It is with another person. On the other hand, suppose I express, "During the past week you received at least five phone messages that you didn't pass on to me [*What happened*]. I am angry and disappointed with you."

Now the power of my emotions is with me. I am choosing to be angry in response to an event. We are potent when we fully assume responsibility for our emotions and needs. The event may be the stimulus for my feelings of annoyance and anger, but that event is not the cause of my emotions. The cause is my choice to respond to the event with those feelings. As Greek philosopher Epictetus once noted, "People are disturbed not by things, but by the view they take of them."

Effective communication involves recognizing that we are responsible, in the sense that we are *able to respond* from amongst a wide range of options, for how we feel and for our actions. Many emotional and behavioral responses are available to us, and in each situation we choose our response. Assertive communication incorporates language that reflects our consciousness of responsibility. Use of "I" statements is an amazingly valuable communication skill. Rather than the editorial "we" or "you," this can generate a transformation of consciousness. For example, instead of saying, "You know how people feel comfortable when there is really someone listening...," if I assert that, "*I feel* comfortable when someone listens to me," my speech becomes captivating, because I am asserting something about myself.

After expressing *What happened* and her *Inside feelings and thoughts*, Lisa may want to pause and invite Robert to respond. If he does, this could be a good opportunity for Lisa to use her listening tools, thus entering Robert's world and showing that she understands what he is saying—as well as the feeling behind his words—even if she doesn't agree with him or accept what he is saying.

At some point in the conversation Lisa expresses her *Needs and wants*. Here too, "I" statements are useful. "I want our relationship to be harmonious and amiable. For this to happen I need to feel respected, and for you to honor your agreements." With *sattvic*, assertive communication, Lisa's primary intention is not to get her way, nor to make Robert wrong. It is to establish and cultivate a relationship based on integrity, respect and empathy. She trusts that in such an atmosphere, everyone's needs will be fulfilled.

Reading this, some of you may be thinking, "This sounds nice in a classroom, but the world doesn't work that way." Perhaps you are envisioning various uncivil, unproductive reactions from Robert in reaction to Lisa's smoothly presented WIN strategy. Suppose Lisa communicates assertively. Does this guarantee that her husband will respond in a candid, civil and constructive manner? No, it does not. It does, however, maximize the possibility that Lisa will create a meaningful conversation about the issues disturbing her. Passive or aggressive modes are unlikely to produce satisfying dialogue. With assertiveness, Lisa expresses her perspective in a way that is not intended to damage Robert. This maximizes the possibility that he will understand her, and that, feeling safe, he will accept the invitation to express himself and enter into discussion. People tend not to hear our pain when they feel blamed and criticized.

WIN is a technique to convey assertiveness. It is important not to confuse the substance with the form or technique. For example, even if we say words that are consistent with the framework of WIN, we are not being assertive if we do not convey respect for the other person. Similarly, even if we express ourselves utilizing the WIN technique, we are not being assertive if, for example, we are mumbling, unclear and conveying a sense of weakness. That said, form can serve substance, and the WIN strategy can assist us in effective assertive expression.

Each component of the WIN strategy is in itself an effective tool for assertive communication. This strategy can be used as a complete whole, though sometimes it will prove most effective to use its individual parts, such as simply using "I" statements to express feelings, thoughts and needs. Often, clear and objective expression of *what happened* is by itself a valuable communication tool. For instance, when I say, "You procrastinate in taking care of your household responsibilities. I am upset and angry about this," I may think that I am impartially expressing *what happened*. Actually, "procrastinate" is my evaluation of the other person. Instead, an objective statement might be: "Yesterday evening, and also last Saturday evening, you prepared dinner for you and your friends. You left the dishes out overnight, and cleaned them by noon the next day. I am upset and angry about this. I ask that you respect our house rule to do the dishes before going to sleep."

Integrity and Boundaries

To assert ourselves means to know ourselves. If I want to assert myself I need to know what I believe, what I feel, what I think and what is truly important for me. Thus, assertiveness is indispensable for a life of spiritual integrity. In examining my core principles, beliefs and aspirations, it is important to distinguish between what I think should be my principles, feelings and values, and what my actions actually reveal them to be. Such awareness is an important part of the process of spiritual development and genuine assertive expression.

Even if Robert's reaction to his wife's assertive expression is some form of fight or flight, Lisa's assertiveness has assured that she is in her integrity. She has expressed her truth with courage and sensitivity. Our responsibility is not to change others—though with our assertive expression they may change. Our responsibility is to assert our own truth in a manner that respects the rights of others.

Additionally, with assertiveness Lisa establishes boundaries regarding how she is and is not willing to be treated. It is said that we teach people how to treat us, and with assertive expression we consciously give lessons on what we are and what we are not ready to tolerate. Personal power, including the ability to create satisfying boundaries, comes from effective communication.

Non-judgmental understanding is a valuable commodity. As you become a better listener, you may find that more and more people seek you out. This itself can present a challenge, one in which it is important to know how to establish personal boundaries. Being assertive means that we are able to maintain healthy boundaries that prevent us from becoming jaded, drained and of little use to anyone, without building walls that isolate us from others.

Knowing how to say no is an essential tool in creating boundaries. Influenced by a desire to please people and to be liked, we may lack the assertiveness to say no when we really want to. Let us keep in mind that if we say yes to something, we are implicitly also saying no to other things. For example, if I say yes to working overtime, I may be saying *no* to family or recreation time. Perhaps I am saying *yes* to fear of losing my job.

Proficiency in assertive expression keeps us energized and continually inspired to relate, give and contribute. Research among helping professionals has led to the development of a new field of study: *compassion fatigue*. This phrase refers to feelings of depletion from constantly absorbing the pain of others. Immediately following a traumatic event, such as a natural disaster or a violent attack, a team of helpers, including doctors, counselors, nurses and social workers, is sent to the scene. Nowadays, as a matter of course, a few days later a second team of mental health professionals is dispatched to address the compassion fatigue of the *first* team. It is understood that after being present for and intensely absorbing such intense grief for several days, many persons will naturally need intervention. This recognizes the importance of having sound boundaries in place when it comes to emotionally charged exchanges, and indicates the value of assertive communication. Preserving boundaries is integral to steadily participating in life and relationships with joy, appreciation and compassion.

EXERCISES

Exercise 1

For the statements or descriptions below, indicate whether they are most characteristic of passivity, assertiveness or aggressiveness.

1. "I have confidence in my own judgment."

2. A person finds it very difficult to make decisions.

3. "I have been working here for three years and my record is very good. My sales results and customer service ratings

are in the top 10 percent of the company. I feel upset because I have not had a raise. I think I deserve a raise."

4. A person nervously avoids eye contact when speaking with another.

5. A person often finishes others' sentences for them.

6. A family member shows anger with obscenities and name-calling.

7. A committee member is reluctant to speak up in a discussion.

8. A friend is able to refuse requests from friends that he believes are unreasonable.

9. A person who is disturbed by someone smoking near her is able to say so.

10. A person often avoids people or situations because of fear or embarrassment.

Here are my responses for Exercise 1:

1. Assertiveness

2. Passivity

3. Assertiveness

4. Passivity

5. Aggressiveness

6. Aggressiveness

7. Passivity

8. Assertiveness

9. Assertiveness

10. Passivity

From the exercise above we are able to glean further distinctions between the consciousness of passivity, aggressiveness and assertiveness. For example, the ability to comfortably look directly at a person when we speak, in a non-threatening manner, is an indication of assertive nonverbal behavior. Of course, the meaning of nonverbal behavior needs to be considered in the context of culture. Still, it is often true that an overly passive person, controlled by fear, is unable to comfortably make eye contact. Also, while the passive person timidly withdraws from confrontation, perhaps eliciting lack of respect from others, the aggressive person is offensive in expression, displaying intolerance or hostility that antagonizes others. The cockiness of aggression is not true confidence. It is the flip side of passive insecurity. Assertive behavior enables a person to act in his or her best interests, without undue anxiety, exercising personal rights without denying or trampling on the rights of others.

Exercise 2

Circle the number in front of any statement where you consider that the speaker is assuming a responsible stance for his or her feelings.

1. "I feel hurt when you say I have no brains."

2. "I feel fortunate that you helped me with my assignment."

3. "I am never listened to around here, and that makes me angry."

4. "You said you would finish your homework yesterday and you didn't. You've disappointed me again."

5. "I am happy that I have been recognized for my achievements at work."

Here are my responses for exercise 2:

Numbers 1, 2 and 5 are statements where I consider that the speaker is assuming a responsible stance for his or her feelings. In scenarios 3 and 4, the speaker seems to be giving his power, or responsibility, to others; this leads to a feeling of disappointment or anger.

Exercise 3

Apply the WIN strategy in three relationships in your life during the next week, and write a few lines noticing your experience in utilizing this communication approach.

FEEDBACK

Personal and interpersonal development is founded on effective communication, and much of communication assumes the form of what we sometimes call "feedback." In listening with empathy we implicitly send feedback that says, "You matter. I am interested in you." Our nonverbal communication is feedback for people around us. Being assertive and utilizing the WIN strategy of communication sends feedback about acceptable boundaries. In receiving an assertive statement I get to hear how my actions are affecting others. Assertively giving feedback is compassionate, showing that you care enough about the relationship to express the truth. Here are some additional varieties of feedback that are conducive for personal development and growing relationships.

Immediacy

Immediacy is an important interpersonal tool that provides valuable feedback and requires assertiveness. With immediacy, we engage in direct talk about our relationship with the person with whom we are speaking. Often in relationships we talk about things happening outside the relationship, and certainly there is a place for that. Willingness and skill to engage in "you-me" talk—direct talk about the relationship itself—is especially enriching and conducive for high-level interpersonal relating.

An immediacy statement could take the form of expressing your experience and perception of the general state of the relationship. "Often we seem to really aggravate each other. Maybe it will be helpful to talk about this." "I am feeling uncomfortable that you seem to need my permission so much. I have allowed myself to assume the role of granting permission. I'm worried about this dynamic between us." Psychologist Carl Rogers speaks about utilizing direct talk to effectively challenge a client:

> I recall a client with whom I began to realize I felt bored every time he came in…Because it was a persistent feeling I realized I would have to share it with him…So with a good deal of difficulty and some embarrassment, I said to him, 'I don't understand it myself, but when you start talking on and on about your problems in what seems to me a flat tone of voice, I find myself getting very bored.' This was quite a jolt to him and he looked very unhappy. Then he began to talk about the way he talked and gradually he came to understand one of the reasons for the way he presented himself verbally. He said, 'You know, I think the reason I talk in such an uninteresting way is because I don't think I have ever expected anyone to really hear me.' We got along much better after that because I could remind him that I heard the same flatness in his voice I used to hear.

The tool of immediacy can also be used to address what is happening on the spot. "You seem hesitant to talk with me." "I've noticed that we seem to be dancing around the issues in this conversation." "Just now, as I started to speak about my promotion, you folded your arms and looked down at the ground. I'm wondering what message you are sending to me with that."

Immediacy statements demand the courage to be genuine and vulnerable. Also, they require competence in other communication tools, such as empathy, attending behavior and "I" statements. In presenting expressions of immediacy we want to be tentative in our language, because our comments may touch on sensitive areas, and while the effect can be confrontational, we don't want to be intimidating. Tentativeness can include phrasing such as "Perhaps...," "It seems to me...," and "It is my impression that..." Because of the challenging nature of immediacy, it is important to ensure that we have built a level of trust—perhaps using tools such as reflective listening and open-ended questions—that can contain the use of immediacy. Otherwise, our attempt at this skill may prove to be a roadblock. Effective use of immediacy requires awareness of what is happening in the relationship, accompanied by sufficient psychological distance to empathically and assertively respond to uneasy patterns or moments.

When we share an immediacy statement, such as, "I feel very respected by the way you've listened to me just now," or "I'm feeling uneasy and tense with you, like maybe I said something that offended you," we convey valuable feedback while exploring our relationship with another person. Immediacy not only shines light on our relationship, it also provides a perspective for the other person to see patterns in other relationships. If I experience someone as manipulative, mechanical or amazingly inspirational, I may not be the only one in the person's life who perceives him or her in that way.

Immediacy is beneficial for diffusing tension or mistrust in relationships. "I feel my body getting tense in this talk with you, and you seem annoyed by anything I say. Yet, we're both smiling as if everything's okay." "I sense that it's still hard for you to trust me since I didn't show up for that appointment we had two months ago." Other uses for this relationship skill include directly handling attraction or repulsion between people, and addressing barriers to clear relationships. "There seems to be some indication that the fact that I earn more money, even though you've been at the company longer, is causing us both to be uncomfortable with and avoid each other."

Without the capacity for "you-me" talk, relationships become blocked, with the participants fearful to speak about or even acknowledge what is stifling expression. That which is bottled up may surface in forms such as hostility and withdrawing. Below we examine another type of relationship feedback that is useful for clearing and cleaning the relational environment.

Withholds

Spiritually based relationships involve clear and clean relations, where communication openly flows. If we sense a relationship is not clear, this is an opportunity to share another type of feedback, a *withhold*. A withhold is anything that is blocking a clean exchange between me and another person. In order to meaningfully support each other in our spiritual progress, it is important that we are able to communicate with each other at a deep level of honesty. Sharing and clearing withholds is an excellent way to cultivate and maintain healthy, satisfying relationships. A withhold may be a judgment that I think you have about me. Or it could be a judgment I have about you. A withhold could be based on an attraction that intimidates me. Or I could have a withhold with a person because he reminds me of someone in my life with whom I have difficulty.

To clear a withhold is simply a matter of concretely putting on the table the nature of my blocked energy.

"My withhold with you is that I fear you will reject me if I openly express my affection, and therefore I am shut down to you."

"My withhold with you is that I am hesitant to be open with you, because you have interrupted me so many times when I have tried to speak."

"My withhold with you is that you seem fragile to me, and thus I keep my conversation with you superficial."

"My withhold with you is that because I admire you, or who I think you are, I am uncomfortable and nervous around you."

"My withhold with you is that I am reluctant to approach you, because you seem to me to be aloof."

"My withhold with you is that I feel jealous of the way you captivate the attention of people, and I have been afraid that you'll notice my jealousy."

In identifying and sharing a withhold, I accept responsibility for the energy that is blocked between me and the other person. I am not blaming anyone. Rather, I am recognizing and honestly sharing about why my exchange of communication is hindered.

Exercise

Identify and share at least three withholds that you have with people in your life. After sharing the withhold, enter the other person's world, or allow this person to enter your world, and engage in empathic dialogue for at least twenty minutes.

As you may be experiencing in the practice of assertive self-expression and sharing withholds, to create fulfilling and satisfying relationships requires allowing the expression of plenty of dissatisfaction. Consider the example, provided by Drs. Kathlyn and Gay Hendricks, of a water faucet that has not been used for years. When we first open the faucet, the stuff that comes out may be dirty and contaminated. After a while though, clean, clear and tasty water flows out. If we continue to block the muddy fluid, we also block the desirable liquid. Similarly, preventing the expression of emotions that may be unpleasant also impedes our experience of joy, power, connection and other qualities of the spiritual self.

Devoid of the Propensity to Criticize

We may resist the WIN strategy or sharing withholds because of fear that the other person will feel criticized, be angry, or reject us. In some circles it is believed that spiritualists do not criticize. When we picture a saintly person we certainly do not imagine a bitter faultfinder, gossiping and constantly maligning others. At the same time a policy claiming that good, humble, spiritually minded people never criticize can be used to stifle honest, authentic expression and engender a culture of fear and repression in the name of spirituality.

The *Upadeshamrita,* or *Nectar of Instruction*, a book from sixteenth-century India, provides an interesting perspective on this subject. It explains that an advanced spiritualist is "completely devoid of the propensity to criticize others." In material consciousness we have a tendency to want to criticize others, to minimize them so that we feel better about ourselves. This is the principle of envy. A true spiritualist has no such inclination. At the same time, a self-realized person is awake and fully conscious. He does not deny his perceptions. He is keen to differentiate between reality and illusion, internally, interpersonally, and socially. If he chooses to share his perceptions, he does so assertively, with compassion, for the purpose of illumination and personal growth.

Attitude of Gratitude

Suppose we hear comments from another person about ourselves. Even if these comments seem completely inaccurate to us, we can appreciate the value in knowing that someone, perhaps representing many others, perceives us in that way. With such information we can adjust our presentation (which is different than compromising our genuineness) so that the perception people have of us is consistent with what is inside us. If the feedback we hear does strike a chord, perhaps causing us to react, then that may be an indication of an area for productive introspection. Even if the delivery of the feedback was not as caring and compassionate as we might have preferred, and even if we suspect that the comments significantly reflect on the other person's issues, still we can use the observations for our own self-realization.

Accepting constructive feedback with an appreciative spirit, we are grateful that this person cared enough about us to be honest. Similarly, by our willingness to share honestly with people in our life, we give them the opportunity to respond honestly to us, to who we actually are. Otherwise, relationships degenerate to a pretentious exchange designed to maintain shallow, false facades, at the expense of vitality and the spiritual fulfillment that results from genuine reciprocation.

There also exists *directly appreciative feedback*, where we share with each other about qualities and behaviors that inspire and move us. In sharing appreciative comments it is especially enriching to be concrete, to specifically state what it is about the other person that we value and admire. For example, to say to someone, "You taught a good class" is not particularly concrete. In fact, it could be considered to be a judgment. Although it may be regarded as a positive judgment, it still may be a barrier to communication—just as much as a negative judgment is. This sort of compliment does not provide the receiver with as full an experience and understanding of thankfulness as a statement such as: "When you spoke about and demonstrated empathy, and about people not caring what we know till they know that we care, and about the power of completely entering the world of another person, I sensed worlds of possibilities open up for me, and felt so hopeful and grateful to be alive. I teach high school students, and this workshop has provided me so many exciting tools and principles to enhance my service to my students." With such a statement the receiver clearly knows what he did that was appreciated, and how the person felt as a result.

Expressing appreciation in *sattva guna* means that our intention is to celebrate the life-enriching qualities of others, with no motive to manipulate or coerce, or to fulfill some personal agenda. Such *sattvic* gratitude is a cornerstone of spiritual life. Research has demonstrated that an attitude of gratitude is a key element of a fulfilled life. Philosopher Sam Keen wrote, "The more you become a connoisseur of gratitude, the less you are the victim of resentment, depression, and despair...The sense of gratitude produces true spiritual alchemy, makes us magnanimous—large souled." Practicing gratitude, intentionally being thankful, transforms how we view and experience the world. It infuses us with power to convert our most challenging times into sources of meaning and inspiration. Consciously being grateful and expressing thankfulness connects us moment-to-moment with the spiritual self's sense of wonder and discovery. In giving appreciation we responsibly participate in the celebration and experience of life.

Receiving appreciation is also a wonderful opportunity to give to people. It is a chance to recognize that we contribute to joy and well-being, that we can be an instrument for the supreme spirit to nurture the lives of others. To receive gratitude in a *sattvic* manner means that we avoid snares such as feeling superior and arrogant, or denying that we are deserving (which deprives others of the fulfillment of having their appreciation gracefully received).

Exercise 1

Each day for the next month, list three blessings in your life.

Exercise 2

Using principles of responsible and concrete communication, express appreciation to three different people for whom you are grateful, and from whom you have been withholding your feelings of thankfulness.

Whether we are sharing appreciation, withholds, immediacy or any other type of feedback, it is helpful to remember that we are probably saying as much or more about ourselves as about the other person. There is a Sanskrit proverb, *Atmavan manyate jagat*, that means, "What we see in the universe, we possess in ourselves." Thus, there is much opportunity for self-discovery in our perceptions of others. Though our comments about others might reveal truths about ourselves, this does not mean that we should withhold honest feedback. As we have seen, we can serve each other meaningfully by expressing ourselves. At the same time, when sharing our experience of others, we can also productively ask ourselves, "How is what I am saying also true about me?"

CREATING WITH OUR WORD

"In the beginning was the Word." Thus starts the famous Gospel according to John. Many great wisdom traditions state that sound—represented by the word—lies at the basis of creation. Just as the supreme creates with his word, we too, as parts of the ultimate source, create our lives with our words. In the Vedic tradition, *The Nectar of Instruction* describes principles and practices for spiritual development; it concludes with a depiction of the most elevated and transcendent consciousness. As a testament to the transformative power of our words, the opening sentence of *The Nectar of Instruction* emphasizes the need to cultivate the habit of controlling our words for anyone interested in spiritual process and profound spiritual realization.

An important aspect of the courses that I conduct is becoming aware of our relationship with our words, of their effect on our life and relationships. The following is an exercise used in the course that will help you to enhance this awareness.

Bring to mind a time when someone made an agreement with you, broke that agreement and afterwards saw you face-to-face. Connect with this experience. Write down two or three words describing what this experience was like. Next, bring to mind a time when someone made a commitment to you, kept it and afterwards saw you in person. Again, connect with this experience, and on a separate list write how that felt.

Now think of an example when you made an agreement with someone, broke it and afterwards saw the person face-to-face. Connect inside, and write a few words describing that experience. Lastly, recall an instance when you made a commitment with someone and fulfilled it. What was that like? Write it down on a separate list.

Typically, the *"broken agreements"* lists include experiences and feelings such as disappointment, hurt, embarrassment, anger, lack of dependability and confusion. In the *"kept agreements"* column we characteristically find words such as trust, gratefulness, responsible, fulfillment, security, clarity, respect and honor. The purpose here is not to moralize about the importance of keeping our promises. It is simply to realize how our relationship with our word affects our experience of life. When we violate our word, then our confidence and trust tend to decrease, and feelings like resentment, distrust and pain predominate; whereas when we honor our agreements, confidence and trust increase, and we develop an experience and environment of appreciation, affection and harmony.

Dr. William Silen, chief of surgery at Boston's Beth Israel Hospital, tells his residents, "I don't know what the difference is between 'major' and 'minor' surgery. I just know that no one performs 'minor' surgery on *me*." Similarly, I would like to suggest that there are no "big" or "small" agreements. Let's say, for example, that I tell you, "I'll call you tomorrow," but I neglect to call. We may think, "Well, it's no big deal." With respect to our relationship, however, the consequences from the *broken agreements* list are likely to manifest. It is probable that your trust in me will to some extent diminish, and our relationship will feel less pure and balanced. Imagine putting a grain of sand in the carburetor of a car. The car will run fine, with apparently no effect. Make a habit of putting a grain of sand per day in the carburetor, and after a year or so, you have a broken car. In the same way, if we make a habit of not doing what we say we will do, we find that after some time we have broken relationships, a life that doesn't work.

In workshops I sometimes ask, "If you keep at least 60 percent of the agreements you make with other people, stand up." Usually about 80 to 90 percent of the people stand. After asking everyone to sit, I will then ask, "If you keep at least 60 percent of the agreements you make with yourself, stand up." On average, 10 to 20 percent of people stand up. We tend to think that if no one is witnessing our commitments, they are less important. However, if we honor agreements with ourselves—to rise early, to stop smoking, or to watch less television—we can expect experiences in the *kept agreements* column. Self-trust and confidence will increase, and we will feel clear and confident. Conversely, not honoring commitments to ourselves will give rise to the items in the *broken agreements* column.

Some of us may carry in our subconscious an equation that looks like this:

Keeping Agreement =
Not Keeping Agreement + A Good Story

And this formula has corollaries, such as:

Being on Time = Not Being on Time + A Good Story

We could think of instances of a broken agreement when the adverse consequences discussed will not occur, where the "good story" side of the equation may actually be greater. Suppose you have agreed to be somewhere at 9 a.m. You stop on the side of the road and save someone's life, and arrive at your appointment at 10 a.m. Did you keep your agreement? No, although perhaps in this exceptional instance the unpleasant results usually attending violated commitments will not happen, because you served an even higher principle.

It is not that one side of the equation is always greater than the other. It is simply that it is not an equality.

Keeping Agreement ≠
Not Keeping Agreement + A Good Story

Being on Time ≠
Not Being on Time + A Good Story

I suggest, though, that for the vast majority of occasions when we transgress our word, harmful effects materialize. Our "good stories" for not honoring agreements are rarely in fact "good stories"—and our justifications don't negate the unpleasant experiences. More than 99 percent of the time, respecting our word creates a more satisfying experience of life and relationships than breaching our promises. And the reality is that, unless there is some calamity, most people don't particularly care about the reason that we did not fulfill our commitment to them.

Personal growth involves making challenging commitments and then honoring them. If we are not creating commitment in our lives, we may not be sufficiently stretching ourselves to expand our limits and possibilities. When we give our agreement, we will probably find that despite our best efforts we sometimes don't follow through. A strategy for handling broken agreements with integrity is therefore a valuable tool for spiritual transformation and restoring relationships.

A strategy I use in my seminars and in my life is called *The Five A's*. The Five A's are 1) Acknowledge, 2) Accept responsibility, 3) Account, 4) Apologize, and 5) Amend.

Handling Broken Agreements

1. Acknowledge

2. Accept responsibility

3. Account

4. Apologize

5. Amend

Acknowledge means recognizing that we have broken an agreement, and expressing this acknowledgment to the person whom we have transgressed against. We are not justifying, defending or rationalizing the broken commitment. Acknowledgment includes empathetically understanding the pain, disappointment, loss of trust and other emotions we may have caused by violating our word.

The second A, *Accepting responsibility*, denotes realization that I responded in a particular way—or neglected to respond in a particular way—that resulted in not honoring my word. By accepting responsibility and expressing this to the person to whom I broke my commitment, I save myself from playing the blame game.

The third A is *Account*; my expression of accountability involves genuinely explaining what happened. Explanation does not mean defense or excuse. A truthful explanation may sometimes show us in a positive light—such as the example where we save a life at the expense of keeping our word. Often, though, our explanations are unflattering, such as "I spaced out about our appointment because I was watching television," or "I paid a few bills instead of paying my debt in a timely fashion."

Apology is the fourth A, and it is important to note that it is fourth, not first. Often we act as though apology is the first and only step in effectively handling a broken agreement. "I'm sorry" can be more about my need to look good and restore my image than about sincerely expressing remorse and reinstating the soundness of the relationship. Even more, we can imprudently use "I apologize" as implicit permission to do the same thing again. Without acknowledging what we have done, accepting responsibility and honestly accounting for it, the apology may be hollow. Following the first three As, apology is a natural step in managing broken commitments.

Amend is the fifth A; this means doing what we can to redress the situation. We may approach the other party for ideas for righting the relationship, while being conscious of not putting the burden of responsibility on them.

Through making and keeping agreements, we grow and strengthen our relationships. Each of us can identify things we could and should do to better our lives. As an exercise, before the end of your day today make a commitment, keep it, and notice the experience.

A key element of trustworthy character is being a person of your word. Cultivating this trait is beneficial across the spectrum of our lives. Each commitment we keep, to ourselves and to others, is powerful, reinforcing our credibility. Creating trust in our words is an essential component of the sacred space that engenders confidence, closeness and a safe environment for personal exploration and development.

PART THREE

Be-Do-Have:

A Paradigm for Conscious Living

Alternative Perspectives

"Like it? Well, I don't see why I oughtn't to like it. Does a boy get a chance to whitewash a fence every day?"

Thus responded Tom Sawyer to the query of his friend and foe Ben Rogers, who had doubted Tom's enthusiasm for painting his aunt's fence on a bright and beautiful Saturday morning. Certainly Tom didn't enjoy the task at first, discouraged as he was by the thirty yards of board fence nine feet high. Life to him seemed hollow, and existence but a burden. Then, after some failed intrigues to maneuver others to take up the task, Tom had a great and magnificent inspiration.

Ben boasted, 'Say—*I'm* going in a-swimming, *I* am. Don't you wish you could? But of course you'd druther *work*—wouldn't you? Course you would!'

Acting on his inspiration, "Tom contemplated the boy a bit, and said: 'What do you call work?'

"'Why, ain't *that* work?'

"Tom resumed his whitewashing, and answered carelessly: 'Well, maybe it is, and maybe it ain't. All I know is, it suits Tom Sawyer.'"

Absorbing this perspective, Ben soon replied 'Say, Tom, let *me* whitewash a little.'"

By the middle of the afternoon Tom's boyhood fortunes were substantially enhanced, as one boy after the other passed by, eagerly surrendering prized possessions for the opportunity to paint the fence.

This episode from *The Adventures of Tom Sawyer*, whereby Tom realizes the truth in the ancient proverb *If you love what you do, you'll never have to work*, shows that different perspectives create different experiences and different results. The activity may be the same, but the consciousness with which we approach it determines our experience.

In many of the seminars and workshops I teach, we focus on the principle of alternative perspectives in transforming our lives. Once I encountered a woman who had just completed the seminar. She was very excited and had an experience she was eager to share with me. In the spiritual community where she lived she had taken a vow to chant daily a prescribed number of mantras on a rosary. She exclaimed, "This morning I realized that I don't have to chant my rounds! I don't have to chant my rounds!" Her exhilaration filled the air with a sense of liberation. Seeing me rather puzzled as to why she was happy to give up her vow, she went on, "I get to chant my rounds! I get to chant my rounds!" She then explained how that morning she had begun to finger her rosary and chant a few mantras. For the first time in her decades of experience she found herself in tears while chanting. For the first time she wasn't in a consciousness of "I have to chant my rounds." Her meditation was coming fully from choice. She was immensely grateful for the opportunity to vibrate these sacred words.

Another telling example of the positive benefit of changing your perspective is that of the Jesuit priest Walter Ciszek. Writing about his ordeals as a priest in Russian prisons, he reflects on a perspective distinct from those of most other inmates. "The prisoners survived by taking life as it came, rolling with the punches, hoping only to survive each day as it happened, one day at a time. Surely my motivation ought to help me see beyond that. Each day to me should be more than an obstacle to be gotten over, a span of time to be endured, a sequence of hours to be survived. For me, each day came forth from the hand of God newly created and alive with opportunities to do his will. For me, each day was a series of moments and incidents to be offered back to God."

When we unconsciously cling to a particular perspective, we run the risk of limiting our life experience and results, like the frog in the well that thinks the sky is only as big as the top of the well. By coming to the surface the frog gains a different view. We enhance the quality of our life when we bring belief systems and perspectives that may be constraining to the conscious surface.

LANGUAGE REFLECTS CONSCIOUSNESS

Often our language reflects and reveals our consciousness. Tom Sawyer shifted from "I have to paint this fence" to "I get to paint this fence." Accompanying that shift was a transformation from an experience of emptiness, discouragement and burden to one of creativity, enthusiasm and success.

An important aspect of the courses I conduct is that the participants examine their lives from alternative perspectives, and change for the better as a result of that exploration. At the core of this examination are the principles of choice and responsibility. A stance of personal responsibility is the most effective attitude for living a life of excellence and creating the experience and results we desire.

In the seminars we spend time looking at how language affects and reflects consciousness. For example, we consider the expression "I can't" in contrast to "I'm not willing to." Through an experiential process, participants often realize that they use "I can't" to express a sense of disempowerment, whereby the script of their lives is written by external forces, whereas "I am willing to" or "I am not willing to" reflects a consciousness of responsibility, personal power and choice. Frequently I hear participants say that "I can't" feels easier to say, although "I'm not willing to" is more honest.

Several years ago I was conducting couples counseling. In one case a man would regularly lose his temper with his wife. Sometimes this would happen at especially precarious times, such as when they were driving on the highway. Understandably, this behavior damaged the relationship. The woman acknowledged that she had played a part in the situation, provoking him in various ways. The man said, when his wife prodded him with particular statements, in a certain tone of voice, "There's nothing I can do. I can't help it. I just become enraged at her."

I proposed to him a hypothetical scenario. "Your wife has said what she says in the tone of voice with which you are so familiar. She has done that, and it is the moment before you explode with rage. The difference is that this time you know that if you don't lose your temper, you'll receive ten million dollars, tax free. Would you become enraged with your wife?" Some hesitation, then, "Well, if I knew I was getting ten million dollars...no, I guess not."

"But wait a second. I don't understand. You said that you couldn't help it. There was nothing you could do. You just had to get enraged with your wife."

"Yeah, but ten million dollars..."

"Okay, now this is a different ball game. Now I am understanding that you have a choice, and you're choosing to get mad at your wife. You just indicated that you could make other choices, and you're choosing anger in that situation."

As long as the power for his anger is with his wife, or any external factor, there is not much room for progress in addressing this client. Once he acknowledges choice, there is something to work with. "You have choices. How come you're deciding to lose your temper with your wife? What other possibilities are available?"

As director of an international child protection office, I worked with a forensic psychologist who assisted us in designing training for child protection team members. He specialized in therapy for sex offenders. He shared a technique he utilized when the sex offender would not accept responsibility for his actions.

"I was in the room with the girl and I couldn't help myself..."

The therapist would then offer, "Okay, suppose it's the same scenario. You are in the room with the nine-year-old girl. This time, though, the difference is that also in the room is a police officer with a handgun. Would you touch the girl?"

"With a cop there with a gun! Of course not."

"But you said you couldn't help it."

"Yeah but if a cop is there with a gun I'm not going to touch the girl."

"Okay, so you had a choice. You could have decided differently. How come you chose to molest the girl?"

In this way the psychologist helped the offender acknowledge that he had hundreds of choice points, at each one of which he made a particular response, which led to a distinct result. He chose to speak to the girl in a specific way; he chose to turn the doorknob, and so on and so on. At any of these choice points the man could have responded differently and created a different result. Once this person had recognized his responsibility, and acknowledged that his responses (or lack of them) had led to the final situation, the therapist could productively address issues with him.

"Freedom of choice, is what you got.
Freedom from choice, is what you want."

—Devo

Should is a word frequently used to avoid a responsible perspective. How do we tend to react when others tell us what we *should* do? We are inclined to defy, rebel, not want to do it. Our nature is to be autonomous, and we resist being constrained by *should*. If we tell ourselves what we should do, our reaction tends to be the same—to oppose. Even if we do obey, such adherence is usually accompanied by such emotions as anger, resentment and frustration.

I was once working with a client who had been grappling with an ethical and moral dilemma in her life. For years, in various ways, she had been giving away her power of responsibility to various other people, expecting them to resolve her problems for her. Whenever their ideas proved to be ineffective, she always had other people to blame. (After all, it wasn't her idea anyway; they had told her she should do it.) When she tried the same thing with me, I declined to accept responsibility for her decisions, and instead assisted her in identifying her value system. At one point she made reference to guidelines given in a religious scripture that she believed applied to her situation, stating that she "should" follow those guidelines. The ensuing conversation revealed that she was simply setting up the religious scripture as her next object of blame. When the religious guidance didn't work, she would be able to lay blame at the feet of the holy books.

Using an ethical, moral or religious system to dodge our responsibility as human beings seems a misuse of our God-given intelligence. Perhaps a better use of our abilities is to make the following assertion, in both word and action: "I accept as my own the value system described in this spiritual approach to life, and I choose to live my life in accord with these ethics and morals, fully accepting responsibility for the results of these choices."

GRUNGIES AND PAYOFFS

Let us look more closely at this stance of personal responsibility with respect to our emotions. Spiritual traditions maintain that the inherent nature of our being consists of qualities such as joy, vitality, consciousness, clarity, radiance, warmth, compassion, love, connection, confidence, balance, beauty, playfulness, ful-fillment and power. Also, a fundamental quality of the self that accompanies consciousness is self-determination, or freedom of choice.

The following are some emotions that people commonly consider to be unpleasant: anger, confusion, fear, feeling like a victim, humiliation, embarrassment, worthlessness, hurt, pain, sadness, resentment, guilt, bitterness, shame, anxiety, inadequacy, pressure, suffering, jealousy, disappointment, frustration, discouragement. Nobody actually likes to be troubled by these emotions.

Assuming that we have freedom of choice, and that our nature is vibrant, bright, powerful and free, how come we would choose experiences such as depression, bitterness, anxiety, worthlessness, fear, guilt and confusion? Based on my experience with people I can guess that some readers are saying, perhaps instinctively, "I do not choose these emotions." Stay with the premise that we are at choice, that we are the creators of our experience. Even if we don't believe this premise to be true, we can reflect on the idea, saying, "Okay, if it were true that I am choosing these emotions, why would I be doing this?"

If we notice responses such as, "It's just a habit...I am conditioned that way," dig deeper. We form habits for a reason. How come today, at this moment, we choose to accede to emotional habits like resentment, depression or discouragement? Whatever our past or conditioning may be, how come, now, we choose to be influenced by conditioning that results in sadness, pain and repeatedly being victimized?

In the spiritual transformation seminars that I conduct, people frequently, after some initial resistance to the assumption of self-determination, generate reasons such as getting attention, gaining sympathy, feeling superior, feeling right, an excuse for not taking risks, protection, manipulation, maintaining an image, avoiding responsibility and reinforcing and justifying beliefs.

We will refer to the items on the unpleasant emotions list as "grungies," and the items on the reasons list as "payoffs." I want to acknowledge that I was first introduced to these terms as well as several other concepts in this part of the bookk through the Lifespring trainings developed by Dr. John Hanley, Sr. These lists are partial. Each of us could probably think of additional grungies and payoffs. The grungy-payoff connection varies according to one's personality. Some of us, for example, may use depression to get attention, whereas others may use anger or confusion to receive attention. Below are a few examples of grungy-payoff interactions.

Examples of Grungy-Payoff Interaction

For as long as she can remember, Ricky has felt worthless, as if she has no value. She knows this is related to the way her father treated her. Still, in considering why she holds onto this feeling of worthlessness she has realized that she uses it as an excuse for not taking risks, to avoid the possibility of failure and also to get sympathy from others. If she let go of feeling worthless, experiencing instead her intrinsic value, she knows she would be more productive and fulfilled. With the new awareness that she does not have to feel worthless, Ricky notices that she no longer feels intimidated around people whose presence formerly caused her discomfort. Ricky experiences the truth of Eleanor Roosevelt's statement, "No one can make you feel inferior without your consent."

Alan repeatedly finds himself in situations—within relationships, in his profession, and throughout his life—where he is the victim. Looking at this pattern from a responsible perspective, he recognizes that being in a victim role gets him attention, and even admiration, when he dramatically recounts his victim stories.

For more than a decade George has been confused and unclear about whether to commit to a university degree program or start his own business, about whether to remain single or get married. Now, adopting a responsible position of choice, he understands that he remains in confusion to avoid commitment and also to get attention from others, who often try to help him make decisions.

Jan lives in fear. Fear pervades her experience of life. Intellectually she knows that most of her fears are irrational. Reflecting on why she holds onto fear, she acknowledges that it serves her in several ways—such as not taking responsibility for the results in her life and protecting herself from hurt in relationships.

Gail is constantly in anxiety. When challenged with the perspective that "Anxiety is a choice," she realizes that most of her anxiety is not productive. In fact, her successes have not resulted from her anxieties and fears, but despite them. She uses anxiety to protect herself from accepting responsibility that she does not think she can handle. With this new awareness, she begins to consider ways to establish healthy boundaries for herself, without excessive anxiety.

Everyone in Bill's circle knows him as an angry person, irritable and severely agitated at the slightest perception of provocation. Honestly reflecting on himself from an accountable perspective, Bill sees that he has been using anger to get attention. As a small child that was the most effective way to get noticed. This strategy still works, to influence others to notice him, and also to manipulate people to do his bidding. But at what cost? Bill begins to consider the price he is paying in terms of intimacy, closeness and respect for hanging onto this emotional habit.

Stephen holds resentment from mistreatment he has suffered. Previously he never considered that he had a choice about this. Introspecting, and hypothetically accepting that he is responsible for his emotional state, Stephen unburdens himself of much emotional pain by acknowledging that by holding onto resentment he gets the payoff of feeling superior to the person whom he perceives has wronged him. Also, he uses resentment to avoid courageously confronting and communicating with people. Realizing the extent to which he has tormented himself by holding onto resentment, he personally relates to the saying, "Resentment is like drinking poison and waiting for the other person to die."

Karen carries heavy guilt: for the way she treated her parents when she was a teenager, for a financial indiscretion with a friend last year, for immaturity in a romantic relationship a decade ago, for not knowing what to say at the committee meeting yesterday, and for a multitude of events throughout her life. Shame and guilt are major coping mechanisms for her. When asked about her pay-off for guilt and shame, after a short pause she responds that she receives the reassurance of others, who assure her that she is a good person and encourage her not to be harsh with herself. Meditating further, she realizes that she gets other payoffs—namely justifying her beliefs about herself and avoiding responsibility. Like all of us, Karen likes to think of herself as a good person. When she does something (or neglects to do something) that she perceives as bad, guilt serves to validate her virtue. "If a decent person does this bad thing, at least she feels guilty about it." With such a framework of beliefs, one episode after the next would be a catalyst for Karen to accumulate and further entrench guilt and shame.

Responsibility, Guilt and Resentment

Sometimes we confuse responsibility and guilt, thinking, "I am responsible, therefore I am guilty." Actually, it is a common grungy-payoff dynamic to use guilt to avoid responsibility. Instead of honestly looking at my responsibility for what happened, and ways I can rectify mistakes, I feel guilty. Rather than sincerely acting to improve my character and behavior, I feel guilt and shame about my shortcomings.

Guilt and resentment grungies relate to our expectations, as shown in the following illustration.

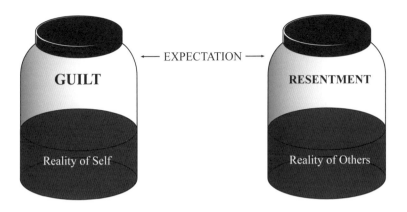

The jar on the left represents your expectation of yourself. The line about 40 percent from the bottom indicates your reality of yourself. Instead of accepting and being satisfied with the reality—or constructively endeavoring to improve your behavior and character—you fill the remainder of the jar with guilt. The jar on the right represents your expectation of another person. The line designates the reality of that person. We have a choice. We can accept that reality, or we can initiate transformative communication towards productive change. But often, instead of making either of these choices, we fill the balance of the jar with resentment. Expectations, or the attachment to them, can be premeditated resentments. Much of our suffering arises from an inordinate desire to control life, insisting that life conform to our expectations. Resisting reality is a losing battle, while surrendering to it brings peace of mind and heart. Surrender does not mean that we abandon efforts to make the world and ourselves a better place. It means that we peacefully accept that life does not always yield to our designs, and that we transcend emotional reactivity to unmet expectations.

Every Emotion Has Its Place

The states of being on the *grungy* list are not always grungies. They have their natural place in healthy human emotional life. For example, suppose someone dear to you passed away, and the next day you felt no sadness or grief. That would be unnatural. Sadness in this case would not be a grungy. Now, imagine that ten years after this person passed away, you are still so grief-stricken that you cannot function, hardly able to rise from bed each morning. That sadness would likely be a grungy, with corresponding payoffs. A grungy is an unpleasant way of being that we do not rectify. We might complain, gripe and grumble about it, but we hold onto it. Here are some other examples of the distinction between natural emotion and a grungy with a payoff.

Many of our fears are unjustified, though we maintain them for payoffs such as an excuse to not risk the possibility of failure, or to protect ourselves. Fear, though, is not always a grungy. There could be valuable messages from fear. For example, if I am fearful of walking in front of a moving truck on the highway, I trust that instinct as a natural protective mechanism, not a grungy that I need to overcome.

We have mentioned *guilt*. Guilt can be an indication that I need to transform or reform my character or adjust my behavior. Guilt can be an impetus for positive change. That is different than hanging onto guilt for a payoff such as avoidance of auspicious change.

For important life decisions there is an expected time period during which we research, consult and gather information. We don't want to act hastily. Lack of clarity for a period of time is natural. During that time, we have a clear sense that we are not ready to make a decision. Contrast that with using *confusion and lack of clarity* to actually avoid making a decision. After we have sufficiently gathered information and experience, whether it is about a career direction, relationship or any other life matter, there comes a time to choose. If at that time we remain indecisive and confused, that may be a grungy with payoffs.

A certain level of stress is motivating, inspiring us to achieve worthy goals. If we find ourselves constantly overwhelmed with stress, however, we may want to consider why we have arranged our life in such a way that stress, pressure and anxiety are so prevalent.

Anger can serve us, protect us and help us establish effective boundaries. Also, anger can be a sign that I have some valuable message to communicate to others—and I can do this with assertiveness, not belligerence. Such expressions of anger are different than holding onto anger and related emotions for secondary payoffs, such as getting attention or manipulating others to feel guilty (which may mean that anger becomes the predominant emotional posture). There is a vital distinction between venting anger in a manner that justifies holding onto resentful feelings and expressing anger in a way that is actually healing, nurturing and empowering.

Just as it is helpful to understand that each emotion has a natural role to play in our lives, it is also valuable to recognize that payoffs are not "wrong." Though in some instances we may want to transcend the need for them, in other cases we may simply want to cultivate healthy and fulfilling ways to get them. For example, I might determine that I want attention and approval in my life, and I intend to receive this through noble actions and accomplishments instead of through anger and guilt. At the same time, I might conclude that I do want to get rid of some of my desire for attention and approval, realizing that much of it comes from neediness that I have been living with since childhood, which is no longer a reality for me. Each of us likes to exert control over his or her environment. If we have been doing this through grungies such as anger or depression, we may consider reducing our need for control, and also generating more productive, straightforward, and beneficial means to exercise autonomy in our lives.

Grungy-Payoff Exercise

Identify two or three of your most common grungies and their corresponding payoff(s). Remember, a grungy is a way of being or emotional state in ourselves with which we are dissatisfied. Even if we intellectually understand the concept of grungies and payoffs, it can be challenging to recognize our own patterns, because we are so close to them. We have found that engaging others in this process can be very helpful. Perhaps form a group of two to six persons who are sincerely endeavoring to enhance their self-understanding and assist each other in recognizing your grungies and payoffs.

GRUNGIES

Pain · Fear · Guilt · Being a Victim · Anger · Worry
Being a Martyr · Anxiety · Sadness · Feeling Bad · Self-Pity
Sickness · Suffering · Tiredness · Jealousy · Boredom
Confusion · Frustration · Depression · Resentment
Humiliation · Disappointment · Embarrassment · Worthlessness

PAYOFFS

Recognition

Attention · Importance · Reassurance · Appreciation
Adoration · Distinction · Approval · Sympathy

Excuse for

Superiority · Failure · Righteousness · Slacking Off
Not Taking Risks · No Accountability

Deception of Others

Manipulation · Leverage · Control · Maintaining an Image

Protection

Maintains & Reinforces Beliefs
Avoidance of Responsibility · Justification

Whether you do this exercise on your own or with a group, while you are doing it, keep in mind the goal—to create positive change. Awareness is the first step in such change, though it is not the goal itself. With this frame of reference, consider how you will *be*, and then what you will *do*, instead of being stuck in the grungies and payoffs with which you are comfortable.

A responsible stance about our state of being is the focus in this grungy-payoff framework. What also needs to be taken into consideration is the influence of our past on our present. The past can certainly explain a lot about our present, but it can not take responsibility for it. Only we can do that. Or at least, a responsible perspective is a very valuable stance in achieving the fulfillment and accomplishments we desire.

This exercise of identifying grungies and their payoffs can also be applied to physical symptoms, such as sickness or tiredness. I have seen many persons rid themselves of physical ailments through assuming a responsible perspective in this area. In making this suggestion, I am of course not suggesting that you neglect proper health care and the guidance of health care professionals. I invite you to try this responsible perspective. Apply it to areas of your life where you are not satisfied, and be open to whatever you may experience.

First We Make Our Habits

This process can be difficult. We are endeavoring to change ingrained emotional and behavioral habits. This requires deep commitment. As seventeenth century British writer and philosopher John Dryden observed, "We first make our habits, and then our habits make us." Conscious living involves examining what our habits have made us, what part of the legacy from our past habits we truly want to keep and what we choose to discard. Hopefully as you read this, exciting prospects are opening up for you. New possibilities can become realities. For example:

"I don't need to be depressed. I choose vitality instead."

"I don't need to live in a cloud anymore. I choose clarity, focus and conviction."

In Part One I mentioned the principle of *subtle leading to gross*. Within this framework we can understand that thoughts lead to feelings, feelings lead to actions, and actions form habits. Thus awareness of our thoughts sets life changes in motion. Grungy feelings originate in self-sabotaging thoughts that counter our spiritual nature. Jealousy, prolonged sadness, anger, bitterness and extreme fear remain in our hearts due to thoughts that deny our nature as content, powerful and balanced beings. And so it is helpful to identify the thoughts underlying the grungies. This is a powerful strategy to restore us to our true spirit. For example, noticing that I tell myself, "I'm useless; I don't matter," helps me identify the basis for feeling depressed. I can replace such thoughts with self-affirming truths about myself.

This is not simply adopting a new belief or opinion. It is about recognizing the reality of ourselves. To know that *"I am valuable. I am meant to contribute importantly to the people in my life and to the world. I am loving"* is to affirm the truth about yourself to yourself. This process naturally inspires us to fully express a sense of responsibility in our lives and not to withhold any of our God-given qualities from our service to the divine. Humility means knowing our position. Denying our qualities means that we are negating gifts from our creator. Acknowledging these gifts and sharing them with modesty is evidence of spiritual integrity. Even with conscious practice we may find that entrenched self-defeating beliefs and grungy feelings appear. Our relationship with them changes, however. Whereas before anger, depression or hurt may have permeated our experience for days or weeks, now the disturbance lasts for maybe an hour or two. We learn to simply notice the under-mining thoughts and feelings, and choose not to allow them to disturb us.

Picture yourself walking on a forest path, enjoying the day. A mosquito enters your space. You could completely preoccupy yourself with the mosquito, giving the insect power to determine and ruin your experience. Or you could acknowledge it, and shoo it away with a minimal amount of effort, while continuing to enjoy yourself.

PULLING THE WEEDS FROM THE GARDEN OF THE HEART

At this point I would like to say something about yoga and its relation to conscious living. Yoga means *to link with the Supreme Spirit*. There are many types of yoga. My own spiritual practice consists of Bhakti yoga, which refers to service with devotion, and is a method of spiritual growth based on connecting with the ultimate spirit through humble and devotional activities of service. An important component of Bhakti yoga is "pulling the weeds"—removing from our hearts any unwanted things, elements that are foreign. In this metaphor, the heart is a garden where spiritual qualities are meant to flourish and blossom. Removing our grungy-payoff habits is one way of pulling the weeds from our hearts, clearing the field so that all the water that enters the garden is used for nourishing the seeds and flowers of the authentic self. Water and sunlight are not misdirected toward the weeds, because we are vigilant not to allow weeds to grow. We are not meant to agonize, smolder and ferment with bitterness, depression and fear. These things, in their grungy form, are foreign elements. Clearing them is an essential aspect of restoring our natural state of fulfillment, balance and power.

To apply this process of pulling the weeds from the heart, I'd like to define a "racket." A racket is *a deception practice that secures gain.* Using a grungy to obtain a payoff is a type of duplicity, or racket, at the expense of straightforward expression and communication. I would like to specifically address grungies and payoffs in connection with our relationships with others. In the context of relationships, we are referring to a grievance about someone else (or a group or organization) that is accompanied by a fixed, grungy way of feeling. That it is a grungy indicates that we are not doing anything productive about it. The price paid for rackets in relationships includes missed opportunities, loss of vitality, loss of health, lowered energy, loss of *aliveness*, loss of intimacy and loss of genuine self-expression.

An Exercise in Relationship

In terms of relationships, to effectively pull the weeds we must stand 100 percent in our responsibility. The other person is 0 percent responsible. This is unconditional. Nothing is required from the other person. We take full responsibility for our experience, and for our contribution to the relationship.

As a recommended exercise, internally accept this stance of 100 percent accountability in at least three of your relationships. Describe your racket to the other person. The racket consists of your grungy or grungies with the person, and the payoff(s) you get from those grungies. Bring the racket from the obscure background to the clear foreground with straightforward talk. This requires valuing being with someone more than being "right" in your relationship with someone. After describing your racket to the other person, make a commitment to them that you will no longer run this racket. Then declare what is truly important to you in your relationship with this person. Do this exercise with complete authenticity, so that the other person is genuinely moved and inspired.

To summarize, there are four parts to this process: 1. sharing with the other person the grungy that you maintain, 2. revealing to the person your payoff(s) for using this grungy, 3. committing to the person that you won't run this grungy-payoff racket anymore, and 4. declaring to the person what is essentially important in your relationship.

Here are some examples:

Spouse to partner: "I sulk a lot so that you will feel sorry for me and stop being angry with me. I will not do this anymore. What's actually important in our relationship is that we create a loving, cooperative spirit in which to raise our children and set a good example for them."

Note that the spouse is not justifying the anger or other behaviors of the partner. This process is not a matter of right or wrong. Rather, the spouse is taking full responsibility for his or her contribution to the relationship. This spouse might still have issues with the partner's behavior. Instead of sulking, however, the spouse could learn a healthier, more effective means to address concerns, such as an assertive statement like "You yell at me and then I feel terrible and hurt, because I don't believe there is justification for your hostility towards me. I would like to discuss these things with you, and it is important for me that your tone is respectful."

Colleague A to Colleague B: "I feel bitter and resentful towards you to justify my behavior of speaking badly about you to our coworkers. I will not do this anymore. What's actually important in our relationship is that you and I are friendly and civil towards each other in order to create a pleasant work environment."

Parent to child: "I get angry with you so that you will not cling to me so much. I won't do this anymore. In our relationship what's important is that you know that I care about you and that you trust me."

Pulling the weeds is taking a stand for the paradigm of 100 percent responsibility. We are not blaming others for our experience in the relationship, nor are we assuming a position of 50-50. We stand fully responsible for our experience, response and contribution.

People often seek payoff for their negative emotional states. For example, suppose a child finds that by becoming sad or angry he gets the loving attention of his parents. The payoff is sympathy and attention. When the child becomes an adult he then has an unconscious habit of becoming morose or furious when he wants to feel loved. Even though there is always an immediate cause for the depression and rage, the underlying cause is this behavioral pattern established in childhood. As the person grows older, and his relations become increasingly complex, the attention payoff he receives in response to his affective displays probably becomes decreasingly satisfying. The attention he receives may be that others become angry with him, or patronize and belittle him when he becomes unhappy. These responses no longer provide the fulfillment he received from the childhood response of parental love. Not conscious of his manipulations however, he increases his suffering because he does not know how to achieve what he really desires in a positive fashion.

Our rackets interfere with the experience that we genuinely desire in life and relationships. We may productively apply this understanding to our relationship with the supreme. It might be fruitful to consider that we avoid our constitutional nature of joy, power, courage, openness, balance and fulfillment by running rackets on the ultimate source—whatever our concept of that may be. Our most natural state is blissful and conscious. These qualities, along with the other radiant qualities of the authentic self, are experienced in connection with the supreme. Many of our grungy states—such as anger, envy and resentment, which we may direct towards parts and parcels of the supreme—may originally be directed towards the creator for various payoffs, such as maintaining a sense of control, being right or avoiding responsibility. Ultimately this leaves us unsatisfied, as the payoffs are secondary, and do not serve the primary needs of the self.

As an example of payoffs being secondary, consider that the self is naturally valuable, and to experience a sense of value is intrinsic for each of us. The payoff of superiority in relation to a grungy such as resentment, however, is a diluted experience of this essential worthiness of the spiritual self. For those engaged in the modes of *rajas* and *tamas*, needing to feel superior through a racket is an attempt to replace the primary, authentic and spiritual experience of worthiness and value. To feel superior we may develop a tendency to criticize others unnecessarily, perhaps accompanied by grungies such as hostility and acrimony. This strategy is employed at the expense of expressing our natural value and gifts in healthy and constructive ways.

By actually expressing our grungy-payoff racket to another person and making the commitment not to use it anymore, we positively involve that person in our personal growth. If we lapse into using depression to get attention, or being spaced-out to avoid responsibility, the friend to whom we revealed our racket is there to point it out and help us progress in cultivating more fulfilling emotional and behavioral habits. St. Augustine observed, "A habit, if not resisted, becomes necessity." To break an entrenched dysfunctional pattern requires that we consciously resist it, and this is facilitated by enrolling people in our lives who can support and challenge us in this endeavor.

In applying this *pulling the weeds* exercise, I encourage you to use it along with the relationship principles and communication skills from the *Sacred Space* chapter. To actually express the four parts of this process may take only a couple of minutes. I recommend that you also set aside plenty of time to address the responses that ensue from your sharing, perhaps utilizing strategies such as WIN (page 66) and empathic dialogue to process the communication that results from pulling the weeds in the heart.

VICTIM STORIES: AN ALTERNATIVE PERSPECTIVE

Each of us has victim stories—stories we have told to others, maybe numerous times, intended to convince them that we are victims. To integrate a responsible position in our lives, transforming our victim stories is very valuable. Here is an exercise to invite an alternative perspective towards these stories.

Identify three significant times in your life when you felt victimized. Describe these in detail, using a separate page for each victim story. Absorb yourself in this process, connecting with the pain of being a victim in that episode of your life. Write as if you are attempting to convince the reader that you were a victim.

After you have written your three victim stories, revisit each narrative and, below it or on a separate page, write the same story—this time from a perspective where you fully take responsibility for what happened. Regardless of whether you believe the accountable perspective to be true, commit to this process with full emotional energy, and simply notice your experience. Write as if you are endeavoring to convince the reader that you have fully taken responsibility for this episode of your life.

Here is an example of a victim story, from my life:

I worked as a foster care counselor in an outlying county. I applied for a position much closer to home, with better pay and involving work that was more fulfilling. A few days after the interview I was notified that I had been offered the new position.

Accepting the job, I gave my two weeks notice to my supervisor at my first job. In the late morning of my final day there, my colleagues in the office arranged a going away party for me. That afternoon I was clearing out my office, excited about beginning my new job at 8 a.m. the next day. At about 2 p.m. I received a call from the new supervisor. She informed me that they were retracting the offer, no longer offering me the job. That was the extent of the conversation. I was devastated, confused, humiliated. I had informed friends and family of my attainment and was embarrassed to consider informing them of this turn of events. In the following days I made some inquiries and discovered that my current supervisor had bad-mouthed me to the new supervisor, and had persuaded the new supervisor to withdraw the offer. I had been slandered, and this hurt very much. I felt powerless, angry and disgraced.

Here is my *accountable version*:

The supervisor who hired me in the outlying county left her position about two months after hiring me. The supervisor who replaced her was already administering a unit in an adjacent county, and was temporarily accepting responsibility for the unit in which I was employed until a new supervisor was hired. I had no prior interaction or relationship with this temporary supervisor. I could understand that she was feeling pressure, having assumed responsibility for an extra department with which she was not familiar. Also, I knew that there was an unwritten convention that one should not apply for a new position till the probationary period of one's current position was completed. In my job, the probationary period was nine months. I applied for a new position after about six months. When I received the offer for the new job closer to home and with better pay, I gave the temporary supervisor two weeks notice. I could certainly understand that my leaving would add even greater stress for the temporary supervisor, because she would need to handle the unit with one less case worker until someone could be hired and trained to replace me.

Additionally, I had heard from persons who had worked for many years with this temporary supervisor that she had a mean and nasty streak. By mentioning this, my intention is not to claim that I was a victim because she was malicious. Rather, I am acknowledging that I had knowledge that she had a tendency to act in spiteful ways. I possessed this knowledge, I comprehended the strain she was experiencing, and I recognized that I was crossing boundaries of accepted etiquette. Still, without additional communication on my part I gave her notice that in two weeks I would be leaving the job. I could have consulted with her before applying for the new job, empathized with her situation and pressures, explained to her my situation and discussed with her how to create a resolution whereby everyone would be satisfied. I didn't do any of this. Understanding what I understood, I could have expected that she would act the way she did. Actually, I had no right to expect a different result. I see clearly how I created the outcome by my actions and lack of actions.

That is my accountable story. And that responsible perspective is true for me. I own it, and it works for me. Notice that in the accountable perspective, I include some facts that are conveniently omitted from the victim story. Often when telling our victim stories we leave out certain details because their inclusion might prevent us from receiving the payoffs that accompany our victim stories. Also, notice that my responsible perspective does not justify the actions of the slandering supervisor. She acted wrongly, and that does not detract from the fact that I fully accept responsibility for the result.

I would like to make a distinction between *being a victim* and *being victimized*. Each of us can identify times when we were victimized or mistreated. That is different from carrying a victim mentality with us through our lives. For example, suppose someone breaks into your home and burglarizes you. You have been victimized. What the intruder did was not right. Naturally there will be some emotional response on your part, perhaps anger, fear or hurt. These emotions could move you to action, such as contacting the police and endeavoring to get the money returned and the criminal imprisoned. As the days and weeks pass, you move on with your life, emotionally and in all ways. You were victimized, but you are not a victim. Contrast that to the scenario where years after the burglary, you bitterly complain to everyone you meet about how the robbery ruined your life and opportunities. In this case you are being a victim, continuing to give your power to the transgressor.

Of course, we could evaluate things at a philosophical level. My belief, for example, is that we create even the circumstances of our birth. This perspective makes sense to me, and it works for me. From that perspective even experiences of victimization, as described above, might not be regarded as such. My intention though is not to minimize the pain of victimization experiences. Where pain exists, it is important to acknowledge it and experience it, without avoiding or denying it through intellectual exercise.

I have worked extensively with youth and young adults who were maltreated as children. Very often through empathy they are able to connect with and release the pain of victimization that they have been carrying. Through such release, they stop being victims. They stop allowing the people who mistreated them when they were six to keep victimizing them, through emotional intimidation and torment, now that they are twenty-six. They have reclaimed their power.

Perhaps they will use this power to seek justice through social systems. Whatever their decision about this, from a responsible stance they act from choice, rather than from fear. In reconnecting with their life power they gain an alternative framework through which to live. They are not able to change the past. They do, however, enlarge their future by transforming their relationship with their victim stories. Blaming others and experiencing inner peace go ill together. Certainly, others play a role in the challenges we face. Our response to those challenges is a gauge of character. We can accept full responsibility for our fulfillment while also holding others accountable for their actions.

I encourage you to experiment with a different perspective in relation to the victim stories of your life, in the same way that you might try on a new set of clothes to see if you like the fit. Be open to a responsible standpoint about these stories, and notice whether it works for you. This is not merely about resolving, "From now on I will be responsible." More than this, it is acknowledging, "I have always been responsible." That is to say, "Whether I realized it or not, I have been responsible for the experiences and consequences in my life."

As an extension of this exercise, share one or more of your victim and accountable stories with one or more people in your life who are either intimates or perhaps persons who do not know you so well. Ask them for honest feedback regarding their responses to your written stories. Were they more convinced by your victim or accountable versions?

INTENTION, CONSCIOUSNESS AND LIVING OUR VISION

Identifying and changing dysfunctional grungy-payoff habits, pulling the weeds in our hearts and relationships, clearing withholds, listening with true empathy and transforming our relationships with our victim stories are some strategies to open the path for spiritually based personal growth. Such purification allows the aspirations of the spiritual self to directly manifest. Two related truths that are key to fulfilling our life vision are clear intention and *consciousness in the result*. These are based on two principles: that external events and behaviors emanate from internal consciousness; and that spirit is a higher energy than matter, in the sense that spirit is animate and can willfully act to influence material energy.

Achieving a result is wholly a function of intention and not dependent on action. If our intention is clear then even if our plans and calculations are not apparently successful, the result will still manifest in our lives. Situated in the power of our intention, our consciousness is in the result. Obstacle consciousness is the view that "If I can overcome my obstacles, such as weak health, lack of money and lack of self-confidence, then I will achieve my goal." Consciousness in the result is a completely different worldview. In this way of being, the result is already achieved. There are no obstacles to overcome. There may be considerations to address in the process of manifesting the result, but these are not obstacles: if our first response does not meet with success, we will find another way to accomplish our goal.

The fact that accomplishing a goal is not dependent on action does not mean that there is no action. We act with clear intention and consciousness in the result. In such a state of mind, even if a particular set of actions does not produce the result, due to our clear intention we will find another way to fulfill our aims. Accomplishing our goal is not dependent on the so-called obstacles. As Henry Ford once commented, "Obstacles are those frightful things you see when you take your eyes off your goal."

To illustrate this principle, I sometimes cite the example of Swami Prabhupad, founder of a worldwide spiritual movement. In 1965 he came to the United States from India, practically penniless and possessing only some copies of ancient Sanskrit literature that he had translated. His biography describes an event shortly after his arrival in New York. He was sitting on a bench in New York and a resident of the city asked him about his life. The Swami responded by describing how he ran an international organization with more than a hundred centers, extensive publication and distribution of books, and thousands of active members and supporters. Although none of this was manifest at the time, and though externally he may have appeared somewhat down and out, he spoke in the present tense. His consciousness was in the result, not in so-called obstacles.

Obstacle consciousness might sound like, "If I'm healthy enough then maybe I'll be able to do this project...If I can get enough money then maybe I'll open some centers...If people come forward to assist me then I can publish some books." As events unfolded, the Swami did encounter intense challenges in many dimensions. Still, due to the power of his intention, the vision described on the park bench manifested. Because of his clarity of purpose, nothing material could thwart the emergence of his vision.

Intention, Being and Divine Will

Reflecting on these precepts, we naturally consider the relationship between clear intention and the supreme power. Does clear intention imply that we, as spiritual entities with potency greater than any material obstacle, are omnipotent, with ultimate control? Johann Wolfgang von Goethe addresses the issue of the relationship between human beings, our power of intention and God. He writes: "The moment one commits oneself, then providence moves too. All sorts of things occur to help one that would never have otherwise occurred. A whole stream of events issues from the decision, raising in one's favor all manner of unforeseen incidents and meetings and material assistance which no man could have dreamed would come his way. Whatever you can do or dream you can begin it. Boldness has genius, power and magic in it. Begin it now."

Similarly, the *Bhagavad Gita* describes five factors in the accomplishment of all action. They are the place of action, the performer, the senses, the endeavor and, ultimately, providence. As the performer, our responsibility is to be in spiritual consciousness, use clear intention and place our consciousness in the result. From a place of clear intention we strive with full commitment to engage our senses and endeavors to achieve success. While this consciousness does not guarantee goal achievement, it does ensure that we are living in integrity as spiritual entities, and that we are situated to maximize the possibility that providence will act through us to manifest the intended result. Acknowledging providence (or super-consciousness), clear intention harmonizes with the precept "Pray like everything depends on God; act like everything depends on you."

A client writing about the interplay between clear intention and non-attachment in her life once expressed, "There is clear intention and the effort to achieve something, but ultimately I need to let go and trust. Then there is a space, and the results just appear. Between effort and results there is a space. This is a place of a mystic secret, magic—something really significant happens there."

I replied: "Contained in the principle of clear intention is the understanding that 'I might not know how it's going to happen, but I am certain it's going to happen.' This uncertainty about the means, within certainty about the result, seems to reference the sacred space about which you write. We may have a plan A and a plan B. Even if all our plans fall through and don't work, still we are clear that the result will occur...It is a mystic process, in the sense that the Supreme Mystic is the personal mechanism to fulfill clear intention. Clear intention is a way of being that honors that divine space between action and result."

These ideas point to the principle of caring and committed detachment in applying transformative communication techniques and spiritual principles of personal and interpersonal development. For example, empathy is a *sattvic* and compassionate way of being that optimizes opportunities for growing relationships that are connected and enriching; being empathetic, though, does not guarantee that the other person will feel understood and cared for. We can apply a similar understanding with principles such as assertiveness, accountability, and consciousness in the result.

We want to be careful about resorting to the explanation, "I guess providence just didn't want it to happen." If outcomes are not as we intended, it is usually productive to examine our own consciousness and consider what may have impeded the result. This mentality fosters humility, innovation and determination, and ensures that whatever the result, we have succeeded in creating a valuable learning experience. To cite Thomas Edison, "I have not failed. I've just found 10,000 ways that won't work."

Of course, this attitude needs to be balanced with appropriate flexibility and openness to changing course. Furthermore, approaching each situation with a disposition for self-exploration and personal improvement ought not to be confused with a mentality of harshly blaming ourselves for perceived deficiencies. Exploring our consciousness to determine where we might enhance our character, behavior, and results is best done in a spirit of wonder, adventure, and self-compassion.

The River:
Boats, Planes and Karma

A client who was deliberating on a tough life decision and noticing patterns in how she approached decision-making once wrote: "Sometimes I wish that someone would take my decision, just decide for me. In decisions I often let 'the universe' decide...I make no decision, and then regret what happens. Practically all the time I'm frustrated, not knowing what I want, and afraid of making mistakes."

I responded: "I hear your anguish, and see that you're looking at your relationship with decision-making. You seem to be sensing that you 'go with the flow' too much, as an avoidance of being fully responsible about your life. Naturally we want to have a balance between being sensitive to indications from 'the universe' and determined commitment for what we deeply want in our life."

To further explore this interaction between healthy expression of self-determination and flowing with the current, picture yourself on a river, floating in a small boat. Sometimes the current is a torrent, sometimes gentle and scarcely perceptible. For stretches of miles the river runs perfectly straight, and at other times it is replete with twists and turns. Occasionally your motion is almost at a standstill, in the reeds and rushes of marshy waters. At other intervals you sweep by the sloping banks in which the river is confined in shifting corridors of aqua green, of flora and fauna, absorbing your vision.

You do not know what awaits you up ahead. There has been no advance patrol providing scouting reports. Perhaps there will be a waterfall, scenery grotesque, magnificent or bucolic. Will the water's movement lapse or wildly accelerate?

Drifting gently, what do you experience? You might be terrified. After all, you do not know what is coming next. Panic is an option. Or, you may experience calm, captivated in this beautiful adventure, secure and trusting in yourself and your capacity to handle whatever comes your way.

At times you are afloat, allowing your boat and body to flow with the river. At other times you paddle deliberately, sometimes subtly steering yourself, sometimes with vigorous effort and increasing pace, in order to avoid approaching crisis. To apply willful intention or to go with the flow is a choice that is always available, and the interplay between the two shapes your experience of life on the river.

Management of this interplay determines the future circumstances that become the foundation for our future choices. We may, for example, assert our autonomy and paddle swiftly, and a minute later encounter choices about how to handle our velocity—whether to speed up and intensify the thrill, or abruptly slow down to avoid a hitherto unseen rock approaching. Or we may choose to simply drift, and a minute later face a choice between peacefully appreciating the setting, or dislodging ourselves from a precarious position into which the boat has drifted. Choices in the present determine karma in the future.

For some people, this concept of karma has a ring of predestination—but the opposite is true. Through our desires and actions we *create* our karma. Some approach a set of rapids from one angle, some from another, some from a distressed position, others from a standing of stability—each case is determined by past choices.

To explore this idea further, let us move from the river to the sky. Suppose I purchase a ticket for a plane flight from Florida to London. By purchasing that ticket and getting on the plane, I have created my karma. Once the plane is in flight, it may be said that I am limited in certain ways, as a result of my karma, which comprises the choices I have made and the actions I have taken, such as buying the ticket and entering the plane. For example, If I wanted that evening to visit my favorite restaurant in Florida, I would not be able to do so because I am limited by karma—by the fact that the plane is in the air over the Atlantic Ocean.

I am not a victim of that karma. I created those circumstances. Even though there are limiting conditions resulting from past choices, that doesn't mean my life is predestined. I continue to possess a multitude of choices and thereby an abundance of possibilities for creating future karma-future potential for my life. On the plane I could sit quietly and read a book, enriching my spirit. Or I could make a productive business contact, resulting in much abundance entering my life for years in the future. Or I could commit a terrible crime, culminating in spending many years in prison after the flight. I am responsible for my karma, for being on the plane and for creating my future. I am the author of my life, with each page I write influencing the next.

Although karma limits us, by cultivating the *sattvic* qualities we change our karma, we step out of our past. Through development of conscious awareness—of our internal, communication and behavioral habits—we alleviate the reflexive influence of our past on our present experience and future possibilities. The *Bhagavad Gita* further elaborates that by fully dovetailing our consciousness and activities with the supreme spirit from which the principles of karma emanate, we completely transcend karmic bonds.

Empathic Application

How do we apply the principle of clear intention? We can demystify this spiritual law by considering that it is already in effect in our lives. If we want to discover our intention regarding our economic situation, we can simply review our bank statements. To learn our intention about body weight, we can step on a scale. We can similarly apply this check to our relationships, career, spirituality or any other area. The universe reflects our intention.

At first this realization may be discouraging. However, we can transform this despondency to enthusiasm by realizing the power of consciously utilizing our faculty of intention. Much of what we have created is through subconscious intentions materializing in our lives. Bringing the subconscious to the conscious surface we empower ourselves to create the lives we desire, to serve our highest purpose, by adjusting our intention. Author Napoleon

Hill put it like this: "The world has the habit of making room for the man whose actions show that he knows where he is going."

Throughout this book you have entertained and assimilated alternate perspectives. For example, you considered victim stories from a different outlook. Approach the principles of clear intention and consciousness in the result in a similar way. Try it on. See if it works for you, practically and without needing, for now, to resolve all possible universal implications of this stance. I emphasize this in case you notice doubts of a philosophical nature arising. Perhaps you are thinking, "What about this or that group of people who are suffering terribly? How does clear intention relate to them?" Clear intention and consciousness in the result are naturally applied (with ourselves and with others) on a foundation of empathy, respect and compassion and are not meant to be misunderstood or misused in a manner that is callous, insensitive or disrespectful.

In my experience as a counselor and coach, and through the personal transformation seminars that I conduct, I have witnessed thousands of people change their lives by living out this profound principle. For years, a certain client had struggled with attempts to lose weight, trying an array of techniques. Shortly after grasping this principle of clear intention, she reported that she had achieved her goal of losing fifteen pounds. She didn't know how she did it. She wasn't aware of any particular plan or strategy that she had followed. She only knew that for the first time she truly became clear about her goal, and placed her consciousness firmly there.

Another woman described how for years she had been trying to sell a certain piece of land. Whenever she was apparently close to selling, something would get in the way. This was a source of anxiety for her. When she absorbed the principle of clear intention, understanding that the consciousness of intention comes from the

soul, she felt freed from pressure, and her land sold almost immediately. The shortest distance between two points is an intention.
Whatever our most cherished vision may be, let us begin it now,
with clear intention and consciousness in the goal.

STRATEGIES FOR LIVING

Self-awareness moves us to choose life-enriching principles by
which to live. We have addressed several of these, such as clear intention, Be-Do-Have, accountability and keeping agreements. In this
section we focus on additional, related principles that ornament
a life of spiritual development. Spiritual principles for personal
growth are universal, so it is likely that they will be familiar to you—
being inherent to your core being. Without actively applying these
principles, existence can become a sort of animalistic struggle for
survival, rather than a purposeful and uplifting spiritual pursuit.

Each of us makes a certain presentation to the world. Sometimes
this presentation is authentic, where what is presented outside is
consistent with what is happening inside; at other times this presentation is not so genuine. We wear masks; we hide behind facades.
One of the spiritual principles of self-development is living from
choice, rather than fear. The process of transforming our relationship with fear is an essential part of our spiritual growth. Though
fear may be present, instead of it being a cue to withdraw, it can be
a signal to step forward and to courageously take a risk. Sometimes
we may hold up masks by choice, such as deliberately responding
that "we're fine," although we don't feel that way, because we simply
don't want to enter into conversation about our troubles. What we
are addressing here is *wearing masks out of fear.*

Masks take diverse forms, as varied as our personalities. There
is the "happy" mask, where we want to be seen as a happy person,
regardless of what may be going on inside. Being "strong" can be a

mask, as can being "the class clown" or "the intellectual." Playing the victim, "the spiritualist" or the helpless person are other facades we wear. What others can you think of?

Of course, each of the masks listed above is not *always* a mask. Each of us has a genuinely happy and joyful side, an authentic and intellectual way of being, a sense of humor, a strong side, a fragile side. It is when we feel we *have to* be a certain way, rather than *choosing* to be that way, that our authenticity is compromised. If I have to appear "spiritual" at the expense of acknowledging to the world (and perhaps myself) desires or emotions that seem non-spiritual, then spirituality is a mask, not a genuine disposition. If I feel I have to show myself to be an intellectual—even though there are times when I would really like to drop that front and be playful, spontaneous or emotionally expressive—then my intellectuality is a mask.

We put up masks because of the fear that "If you knew who I really am, you wouldn't like me or love me." By habitually holding up masks to the world, we risk becoming lost to ourselves. As nineteenth-century novelist Nathaniel Hawthorne noted, "No man for any considerable period can wear one face to himself and another to the multitude, without finally getting bewildered as to which may be the true."

We use masks because we believe that they will bring us recognition, affection and respect. We find though that even if we are successful in obtaining love, caring, and attention through our inauthentic presentation, we are not fulfilled. We're not satisfied because the appreciation and esteem is not for us; it is for a pretense.

Behind our presentation to the world is a shadow side of ourselves. We often identify with this dark, shadowy aspect of our existence—the stuff that we don't want the world and ourselves to notice. Just as the constitution of our masks varies with our dispositions, so too does the shadow mask. Generally it is composed of murky combinations of emotions that we experience as unpleasant or nasty. Fearful of this shadow side, we want to avoid the pain of these emotions, which include shame, rage, fear, guilt, grief, hurt, confusion, and pain itself.

Take a few moments to reflect on your presentation to the world in various environments of your life. What fear-based masks do you wear? What are the constituents of your shadow side?

Most of us spend much of our energy holding up masks and pushing down experiences that we resist acknowledging. To use an analogy from Dr. Phil McGraw, it is like holding a beach ball underwater—it requires a lot of effort to keep it down. After a while we become exhausted. A characteristic of readiness for spiritual growth is that we are weary of holding down our emotional beach balls. That is not how we wish to spend our life energy any longer.

Shining the light of awareness on that which has been in the shadowy corners is a liberating step on the path of self-realization (though not the same thing as indulging in darkness). Renowned psychologist Carl Jung once stated, "Enlightenment is not imagining figures of light but making the darkness conscious." Opaque places in our psyche create a sense of fear of the unknown, with which we live until we courageously face that which we have been avoiding.

Living and Surviving

There is a distinction between *living* and *surviving*. Spiritually based personal growth entails a commitment to living, rather than mere surviving. Surviving is reactive. We are in reaction to the beach ball. Holding our head above the surface, maybe putting on a smile, we show that we are in control. Actually this is just the survival strategy of maintaining the *appearance* of control. Wherever the submerged ball moves, we move with it, not daring to allow it to be seen. It shifts here or there, and we follow. Who or what is in control? Even if we manage with great effort to keep it under the surface, it is noticed nonetheless.

Perhaps we conceal our rage, not knowing acceptable means for its expression. But it comes out in different ways—like our irritability or loss of temper at petty things. It is similar with other aspects of our emotional beach ball—such as shame. Though we don't want the world to see our sense of shame or to recognize it ourselves, it drives our life, pervades our experience and relationships with feelings of inadequacy. It prevents us from fully sharing ourselves.

Strategies for living do not necessarily entail expressing our emotions more, though for some of us that may be the case. For some who use dramatic emotional expression as a method of avoidance, authentic living may mean less emotional expression.

Looking Good

Other strategies for survival include looking good and being right. "Looking good" means that we are invested in an appearance, rather than being authentic. For each of us the inauthentic appearance has different forms, which are explained in relation to our masks. For some of us, looking good might mean showing ourselves as the strong helper. For others, looking good might mean "looking bad"—the rebel, the defiant person who doesn't accept authority. Blindly accepting authority is no virtue, neither is indiscriminately rejecting it.

Most of us resist accepting the fact that everyone has his or her personal worldview with which to assess life. We become hurt or angry when people reject our views or disapprove of our life choices. However, it is also possible to be open to, and respectful of, the opinions of others without giving away power and responsibility for our life decisions. Being the author of your life means honoring your authority to live as you choose, while allowing those choices to be informed by valued insight and guidance from others. Whether we live authentically or not, we will never win the approval of everyone. There will always be someone in whose eyes we don't look good, despite our best endeavors. Accepting this as a certainty is key to peace and contentment.

Confusing Ignorance with Transcendence

Looking good can manifest as *needing to appear spiritual*. This survival strategy can really hinder spiritual development because it prevents us from seeing where we are blocked. For example, if I am attached to presenting and regarding myself in a spiritual package, and part of that package is *being humble*, then I might not be able to recognize when my thoughts and actions are arrogant. I may screen perceptions of myself through the filter of "I am a humble, unassuming spiritual person." Likewise, considering myself honest as a part of my spiritual presentation, I may interpret displays of deception in some twisted way to maintain my belief of myself as an honest person. Or, assuming myself tolerant, I will construe obvious demonstrations of impatience in ways that reinforce my spiritual *looking good strategy*. The weeds don't get pulled because we don't acknowledge they are there, and thus our spiritual life is stunted.

This phenomenon is akin to confusing ignorance with transcendence, which integral theorist Ken Wilber has called "the pre-trans fallacy." Believing that our spiritual practice has liberated us from the qualities associated with *rajas* and *tamas*, we remain in ignorance of what is true. Consciousness of what *is* true about ourselves is *sattvic*, and is a doorway to genuine transcendence. We need to own our emotions and experiences before we can genuinely transcend them.

Even endeavors to water our flower of spiritual devotion serve mainly to nourish the weeds, if we allow our contrived mask of spirituality to thrive. For instance, meditation or spiritual reading can serve to strengthen our mask of spirituality unless we are attentive to clear the weeds in the garden of the heart. Each meditative moment or mantra chanted can reinforce our conception of ourselves as a spiritual person, and reduce the possibility that we will honestly look at internal hindrances to spiritual progress. Of course, watering the seeds of spiritual inspiration is vital, and is especially potent when accompanied by introspectively and courageously removing detrimental weeds.

Being Right

Being right refers to a strategy where what becomes important is being right in the company of, or conversation with, another person, instead of just genuinely being with that person. We get to feel right, superior and self-righteous, at the expense of the closeness, understanding and intimacy we truly desire. Conversation based on the principles of transformative communication is grounded in a commitment to truth, irrespective of whose opinion is being validated.

Being unattached to being right is especially valuable when we actually are in the right. This does not mean that we should deny our insights or compromise our views or expression. Our opinion may be valid, but that does not mean that being right needs to be our focus in the relationship. By letting go of ego struggles that arise from needing to be right, we experience the joy of directly participating and sharing with another person. Also, getting away from being right helps us open up to interesting and illuminating elements of other people's viewpoints, thus making each relationship and interaction a learning and growth experience.

Strategies for living can themselves be the ingredients for our self-righteous programs. One client spoke about her frustration with leaders at her church. She treated them with empathy; yet they were insensitive and indifferent to her. She expressed herself with assertiveness, taking responsibility for her views, responses and communication; they used "you" statements, blaming and condemning. She was committed to everyone's satisfaction when there was a conflict; they were cliquish, narrowly focused on their opinions and on defeating anyone who seemed to oppose them. She applied all the right principles and skills; they didn't. And then she realized that she had been playing the same game as them—albeit more subtly. This was a source of profound spiritual insight and fulfillment for her. She saw the insecurities underlying her need to be right, and was able to access previously untapped reservoirs of compassion and appreciation.

During one session, a client realized how *needing to be right* was the cause of stockpiles of transgressions that he had committed against others. Suddenly feeling the weight of the damage, he exclaimed, "I'll never have to be right again!" The coach then asked him, "Would that be the right thing to do?"

STRATEGIES FOR SURVIVAL

Looking Good

Being Right

Maintaining Appearance of Control

Avoiding Pain

Giving 100 Percent

A life-enriching strategy conducive to the complete manifesta-tion of our spiritual selves is to participate fully in our lives—to give 100 percent. Not showing up fully for our own lives is at the core of self-sabotaging strategies. In fact, it is the foundation of repeating self-defeating cycles, because by not committing fully we restrict our potential to learn through experience. Acquiring wisdom involves granting ourselves the permission to make mistakes through which we are able to learn.

Think of a time when you didn't participate fully, either in a relationship or some other life experience. What did you lose by doing this, and what could you have gained with full participation?

Giving and receiving complement each other. Let us here make the distinction between *receiving* and *taking*. Both receiving and giving are life-enhancing, whereas taking is devitalizing. You probably know people who, in the guise of giving, drain your energy. To be open to receive the genuine gifts offered by others is life-enriching. Consider the people in your life and consider whether they are givers or takers. Association with givers—those who actually support your personal growth—is important for self-actualization. If you find yourself surrounded by takers, it will be fruitful to contemplate how you can transform the situation, by changing these associations or by constructively improving them. Also, let us examine whether in our relationships we are being givers or takers. Are we energizing or enervating?

A term like "experience fully" may evoke images of abandoning one's intelligence or reason. Actually, being fully present includes being completely available with all of our faculties, including the mind and intelligence. Conscious living entails utilizing our intelligence to enrich and inform our experiences. There is a distinction between employing mind and intelligence to enhance our complete contribution and presence and using our analytical capacity as a barrier to experience. Making distinctions and judgments is a natural function of intelligence. Hiding behind those judgments, however, is a survival strategy born of fear, one that limits our experiences, growth and connection to others.

There is also an important distinction related to this point between living *in* the moment, and living *for* the moment. Living *in* the moment means being present, with all our qualities and capacities available. In the *Bhagavad Gita*, Lord Krishna describes a person in this state as being free both from *tamasic* lamentation about the past and from *rajasic* hankering for the future. Situated in the mode of *sattva*, he is satisfied in the present.

This is not the same as living *for* the moment, where we may whimsically abandon good sense for immediate gratification. Conscious and present living includes learning from the past and planning for the future. In so doing, we don't wallow in lamentation, or brood in anxiety. In full presence, we don't let a moment slip by. We are fully available to absorb what life is offering and to give with wholeness. This is the consciousness where principles of relationship and spirituality, such as empathy, accountability and clear intention, are evident. Philosopher and educator Martin Buber wrote, "In spite of all similarities, every living situation has, like a newborn child, a new face, that has never been before and will never come again. It demands of you a reaction that cannot be prepared beforehand. It demands nothing of what is past. It demands presence, responsibility; it demands you."

> Forget the past that sleeps and ne'er
> The future dream at all,
> But act in times that are with thee
> And progress thee shall call.
> —Bhaktivinode Thakur

Urgency is a life-enriching way of being. Urgency does not mean crisis, nor panic and anxiety. Urgency means that we are fully present at each moment. It means that things that actually matter the most are primary for us, and things that matter less don't get in the way of our focus. Living from this place, dedicated to not wasting a moment, we experience the peace and joy that is natural for the soul, whereas living in the future or the past is accompanied by anxiety—because our conscience knows that we are not in harmony with correct principles.

Giving ourselves fully to our experience is not the same as wallowing in a grungy emotion. When we allow ourselves to fully experience something, we feel clean, complete, resolved and ready for the next experience. To wallow in a feeling is a way of holding onto it, rather than letting it go, by experiencing it completely. For example, suppose we experience natural sadness in response to an event. This can be a painful feeling, and we may have a habit of resisting or avoiding that pain. But there is a saying: "What we resist, persists." By not allowing myself to experience the sadness, it stays with me, an aspect of the emotional beach ball that I push down. The more I resist, the harder I push the ball down, the greater the oppositional force. The sadness will call out to be heard, with increasing insistence. Whereas If I allow my grief to run its full course, I experience healing and I free my life force. Permitting sadness to be experienced opens my heart, allowing love to be given and received.

We can apply a similar understanding to other emotions that we have a tendency to resist. Fully experiencing anger is empowering. Frequently we suppress our anger because it is an emotion that we fear. Most societies have stigmas attached to anger, though the emotion itself can be healthy and productive, when effectively managed. Beneath depression is often anger that has been numbed. Sometimes we hear the terms "anger management" or "anger control." In truth this doesn't mean stifling anger, nor does it mean uncontrolled expression of it. If I lose my temper, or if I am regularly irritable and perturbed, then it means my anger is controlling me; I am not controlling it. Anger control means that I can access my anger at will, and express it when and how I want, with the intensity that I choose.

In some of the seminars that I conduct, we do an anger release exercise, whereby participants have a safe environment to connect with and release anger. This is a great opportunity to release a chunk of that emotional beach ball. Commonly someone will say, "But I'm not feeling angry." Often these are the very people who have anger problems in their lives. They tend to be hot-tempered, or testy and impatient. In the seminar, I point out to these individuals that they may be carrying a lot of unnoticed anger and hostility, and it might be permeating their lives.

When we resist anger, it persists in our consciousness and experience. The healthy expression of anger helps to establish functional boundaries, and ensures that we don't spend valuable life force pushing down anger, building resentment and bitterness. Realizing that anger and all other emotions can be accepted (though certain actions must be limited), we can move towards emotional expression in a productive manner. Resisting hurt can lead to armoring ourselves with anger. Acknowledging hurt and expressing it without blame helps to break down that armor and opens us to a healthy vulnerability, where we connect within ourselves to a place of deep honesty.

Suspending Judgments

Suspending judgments is another strategy for living. "Suspending" doesn't mean pretending that we don't have judgments. Suppose I have a judgment that a person is lazy, deceptive and not very intelligent. To deny that I am thinking this would be dishonest with myself. In interacting with this person, I want to notice my judgments, and suspend them, allowing myself a fresh experience of this person. That experience may confirm my judgments, or it may reveal them to be false and shallow. Suspending judgments permits me to enter into each moment with a sense of adventure and wonder.

Lynn was amazed with Daniel. They had been participating in a four-month group leadership training. Lynn, in her early twenties, had some judgments about Daniel, who was in his mid-fifties. He reminded her of her father, about whom she acknowledged preconceptions, including that he was unable to change. During a group coaching session about midway through the program, Lynn shared with us how Daniel had astonished her. She had witnessed a transformation in him, and due to her willingness to suspend her judgments, she had experienced him in a different and more positive light. Because she was no longer invested in her judgments, she did not mentally put Daniel in a box, and she allowed spiritual relationship and understanding to develop between them. Also, as a result of this, Lynn's perspective toward her father turned a corner; she became hopeful, understanding and optimistic toward him.

Abundance

An abundance mentality is a strategy for living. This frame of mind allows us to see possibilities in each situation. A scarcity mentality is the opposite of the paradigm of abundance. Approaching life from scarcity, we focus on difficulties in every opportunity, whereas a paradigm of abundance realizes opportunities in every difficulty. People coming from a place of abundance are storehouses of fresh ideas and exude a natural confidence.

The framework of the three modes of nature described in the first part of this book can assist us in understanding different relationships with abundance. In the mode of *sattva*, I assume that if I act in harmony with principles of integrity and my intrinsic propensities, I will experience abundance in my life. The abundance that I receive, I naturally handle with respect and responsibility, understanding that satisfaction is not obtained by increasingly acquiring material goods through unnecessary activity. In the *rajas* mode I would equate money with feeling powerful and happy—although such assumptions repeatedly lead to excessive anxiety, lack of fulfillment and diminished self-respect. The *Bhagavad Gita* describes a person in this mode as "constantly desiring to desire," without reference to the satisfaction and peace that lie within. Influenced by *tamas*, I would maintain a careless, reckless attitude, using money in a neglectful and wasteful manner—perhaps for addictive and destructive purposes.

An abundance mindset genuinely celebrates the accomplishments, victories and qualities of others. Living from abundance, we realize that there is more than sufficient joy, recognition and resources for everyone. Our sense of self-value is not derived from comparison, but rather from a secure and intrinsic experience of our worth. In abundance, my success is not dependent on the failure of someone else.

A paradigm of abundance actualizes as a win-win approach to relationships. Win-win means I assume that the success of others enhances my success, and my wins contribute to the well-being of others. From a perspective of win-win, I am committed to victory for everyone. Consider the following example. A small company has one vehicle. One manager is responsible to ensure that a shipment is delivered across town by 10 a.m., while the other manager has three clients to visit by the same time. In win-win consciousness there is no conflict or tension between these people. Neither is thinking, "I need the vehicle this morning." Rather, there is a cooperative attitude of, "How can we both fulfill our responsibilities?" Neither manager actually needs the vehicle. What both managers actually need is for the merchandise to be delivered, and for all three clients to be treated with integrity. With the managers brainstorming together for the maximum benefit of their joint venture, they will likely arrive at several innovative ideas that meet everyone's needs.

A win-lose paradigm assumes that if someone else wins, then I lose; or that if I win, then someone else loses. With reference to the above scenario, a manager with win-lose assumptions might think, "The other manager has had use of the vehicle for the past three days. I need it this morning. If he doesn't deliver his shipment on time, that's too bad for him. It's not my problem." A lose-win model of interaction could sound like this: "Okay, you take the vehicle. I guess I'll just give up on those accounts I was hoping for, like I usually do..." (Thinking, "I'll be the loser again. I'm used to it.") Lose-win—rooted in personal insecurity—conveys the message that while your voice and needs matter, mine do not. This attitude is often accompanied by concealed resentment and hostility.

Lose-lose takes things further, where I act to take both of us down, ensuring success for nobody. With this mentality, one manager may view the other as an enemy, and while conceding the vehicle for the morning, may make plans for sabotaging the efforts of the other manager. Other variations of these relationships to success and winning include *play-not-to-lose*, which is a survival strategy focused on *not losing* rather than actually living vitally and winning, and *don't-play*, where my fear of failure prevents me from any chance at success or true fulfillment.

We can conceive of win-lose as a *rajasic* approach to relationship, whereas lose-lose or lose-win mentalities, which require even less commitment than win-lose, are primarily influenced by the mode of *tamas*. Win-win entails *sattvic* consciousness, where we stand for our convictions while honoring those of others. It requires deep commitment because it is founded on a determination that everyone will be satisfied. This requires dedication to high-level communication, where we take responsibility not just for what we say, but for how our communication is received and the effect it has. Win-win synthesizes principles of empathy, assertiveness and clear intention to create profoundly satisfying results both inter-personally and professionally.

As an exercise, consider an area of your life—perhaps an intimate relationship or a workplace scenario—that you know you are approaching from a paradigm other than win-win, and where you sense that your current mentality is not serving you or others well. Perhaps you approach the situation from assumptions such as win-lose, lose-lose, don't-play or play-not-to-lose. Write down the results and experience that would represent a win for you. Next, being in empathy with the other person, write what you believe would constitute a win for him or her. Then, from a consciousness of abundance and clear intention, generate ways to create winning scenarios for both of you. Communicate your insights and realizations to the other person, and invite him or her to share with you.

To summarize, some common strategies for survival are being right, looking good, avoiding pain, maintaining the appearance of control and hiding behind judgments. Life-enhancing strategies include abundance, authenticity, being courageous, suspending judgments, living with a sense of urgency and participating fully in our lives.

STRATEGIES FOR LIVING

Participate Fully · Share · Be Honest
Be Vulnerable · Take Risks · Be Open-Minded
Surrender · Be Accepting · Be Spontaneous
Suspend Judgments · Commit · Trust
Keep Agreements · Be Childlike

PART FOUR

Realizing the Power
of Conscious Living

Personal Achievement Compact

"Letting go of all that lies behind me...
hands outstretched to whatever lies ahead...
go for the goal."
—Philippians, 3:13–14

Be-Do-Have Revisited

This chapter concerns goal attainment. In the chapter *Spiritual Principles of Personal Growth*, we saw that in the Be-Do-Have paradigm of existence our consciousness starts with *being*; *doing* and *having* then flow from *being*. This is the natural creative process that emanates from our being. Have-Do-Be consciousness, on the other hand looks like this: "If I *have* money, then I can buy a house (*do*), and I will *be* happy and content." "If I *had* more time I would write a book, and then I would *be* satisfied and fulfilled." "If I *had* a better supervisor, I would work at a higher level of production, and then I would *be* valued and successful."

In setting and accomplishing life goals from a paradigm of conscious living, the equation begins with *being*. Often we specify the *have* part of the equation, then *do* the work of achieving the goal, but neglect to *be*. For example, suppose I am thinking, "If I have the right companion then I will live the life I desire, and I will be loved, appreciated, and affectionate." In this mode focused on having, the process moves to doing things that we believe make sense to achieve the goal. This could mean going to bars, parties, or perhaps to work or church—all with the intention of acquiring what we don't have. Be-Do-Have on the other hand begins with experiencing ourselves as loved, contented, and fulfilled. With this consciousness we attract into our lives relationships that enhance our being. Experiencing love, power, beauty, clarity, vitality, radiance, and confidence is not dependent on having any particular relationship or external result, although we do invite and attract relationships and successes that enrich the full experience of our being.

Be-Do-Have consciousness is joyful, contented, and powerful from the start. Living these qualities, I naturally do the things that joyful, contented, and powerful people do—with the result that I have things that joyful, contented, and powerful people have. Being compassionate, loving, and confident, I naturally act in ways that compassionate, loving, and confident people act—and thus I have what compassionate, loving, and confident people have. The salient point about Be-Do-Have is not that it culminates in *have*, but that it originates in *be*.

Be-Do-Have is always in effect, whether we are conscious of it or not. If I am being depressed, fearful, and irritable, I will *do* what depressed, fearful, and irritable people do, and *have* the sort of relationships and life results that depressed, fearful, and irritable people have. If I am *being* trustworthy, powerful, and spirited, I will *do* things that trustworthy, powerful, and spirited people do, and *have* the corresponding results, such as extraordinary success and rewarding relationships.

While *doing* and *having* flow from our *being*, they also enrich our *being*. Thus, being powerful, trusting, and determined, I act with power, trust, and determination. This activity in turn enhances my experience of *being*. It is not that my *being* was incomplete before the activity; this is a dynamic process where *being* energizes *doing*, and *doing* nourishes *being*. Activity is generated from inspired being, not from a place of need.

In the Do-Be paradigm, I am in a mindset that believes "In order to experience the qualities of my being, I need to do such and such." That is different than *Be-Do*, where I am living from the consciousness of "I am complete and whole; I am inspired to do these activities, which naturally intensify and augment my experience of *being*."

Because spirit is transcendent to matter, and because the self is more powerful than material coverings, it is possible to choose the qualities of our *being* at any given moment—whatever the intricacies of those coverings. By doing some clearing work, by pulling weeds and watering flowers in the garden, we can prepare the field and thus make it easier to choose *being*. (Without minimizing the value of this work, the choice to *be* is not dependent on the clearing and watering work we have done beforehand.)

For example, before conducting a seminar, part of my preparation is to do mantra meditation for about ninety minutes each morning. This helps me to feel strong, clear and connected. Sometimes that doesn't happen, for whatever reason. I know that chanting before the start of the seminar day is very helpful for me to experience myself as focused, spontaneous, confident and connected; but if it's 9 a.m. and the seminar is about to begin, and I haven't chanted yet, I am not willing to use that as an excuse not to be fully clear, present, and connected. Whatever my preparation work has or hasn't been, I can choose to be weak or powerful, foggy or clear, defensive or open.

Commitment-driven

There is an important distinction between the consciousness of *having* and the principle of *placing our consciousness in the result*. Consciousness in the result is situated on the platform of being. When we place our consciousness in the result, we set the intention as empowered spiritual beings. Then we simply and effectively handle any so-called 'obstacles' that present themselves.

The *having* consciousness is not fixed in *being*, nor does it trust that our being is complete, balanced and whole. This frame of mind lacks the conviction that the intrinsic nature of the self is a foundation and wellspring of all auspiciousness. With consciousness in the result, we are *commitment-driven*, rather than history-driven. *Commitment-driven* means that our vision moves us, inspires our action and connects us with our being. *History-driven* means being limited by our past; our past experiences and results determine and constrain what is possible now and in our future. My past level of happiness, fulfillment, relationship satisfaction and financial success determines what I believe is possible for me now and into the future. Commitment-driven consciousness recognizes that "till now," I may have experienced myself as weak, hopeless, a victim, bitter and limited in my achievements by various beliefs and circumstances; but from now on I am a vibrant, successful, inspiring person who boldly declares and manifests his vision.

This is not a process of pushing down the emotional beach ball while trying to think positively. It is cultivating the habit of experiencing the qualities of our spirit. In developing this way of being, it follows naturally that we fully experience whatever emotion surfaces, without denying or resisting it. Simultaneously, we can apply clear intention to create the experience that we want. While acknowledging and experiencing my insecurity, for example, I can manifest clear intention to bring to life feelings of confidence and security. Or, while recognizing that I am feeling stuck and awkward, I can put consciousness in the result to experience spontaneity and openness.

Being compassionate with yourself is one of the keys to unlocking your being. Empathy means connecting with someone where he or she is—and this includes yourself. By accepting and even embracing that I am feeling frightened, I also open up to my courage. By recognizing my selfishness, I am able to appreciate my giving and selfless nature.

As we become expert in this process we may find that grungy states and rackets that formerly lasted for days or weeks may now only be with us for minutes or hours. Simple remembrance of our spiritual nature is also an effective means to achieve a transcendental perspective of healthy, empathic non-attachment toward whatever emotional drama we may be experiencing. Of course, this is understood in the context that emotions such as sadness, anger and hurt, are sometimes natural, and not necessarily grungies.

In defining our commitments, it is helpful to remember that it's okay to "do our best" in some instances, without specific commitment to a goal. There is an organic process of learning from our actions and reevaluating goals. However, sometimes we want to declare and commit, to ensure that we write the script of our life. Steadfast commitment to a worthy goal moves us to exhibit our finest qualities and reveal the best side of our characters. As Goethe said, "First build a proper goal. The proper goal will make it easy, almost automatic, to build a proper you."

Developing a PACT

With the above principles in mind, we can create a Personal Achievement Compact (PACT) to help us clarify and accomplish our goals. Below are listed several life areas. For each category rate yourself from 0 to 10, with reference to the question, "How satisfied am I with this dimension of my life?" 0 indicates "no satisfaction" and 10 denotes "completely satisfied." Note that a 10 means that you are currently experiencing complete fulfillment in this arena of life. (Which is not to say that this area could not be improved, or that maintaining full satisfaction on that dimension will not require ongoing attention.) You can also split a section into subsections; for example, you could assign an 8 to Environment/Office, and a 2 to Environment/Residence.

- Spiritual

- Professional/Career

- Health/Fitness/Body

- Abundance/Finances

- Relationships/Family

- Recreation

- Learning and Self-development

- Environment (e.g., residence, office)

- Other (anything else not already covered,
  such as writing, travel or special projects.)

For each rating, consider why you gave yourself that score. What makes Recreation a 5, or Abundance a 7? In this way you are taking a snapshot of your life, taking inventory of each area in your life.

Now, focusing on one area at a time, be creative, visionary and playful, as you write in detail about what that life dimension would be like if it were a 10. Then, concentrating on one area at a time, ask yourself what concrete things you could do to increase the rating.

Here is a six-step process for improving life dimensions on which you would like to work.

1. Rate the area

2. Contract (see below)

3. Goal

4. Why it is important

5. How you will feel when you achieve it

6. Action steps

'Contract' means making a commitment to connect with the qualities of your true being, and which are fundamental for achieving 100 percent of what you declare is important for you in this life area. You are making a contract with yourself to live those qualities. For example, in the area of health, a person's contract might be "I am a valuable, disciplined man," or "I am a determined, healthy, and vibrant woman." Each contract is personal.

These examples are provided to give some idea of what a contract may look like. Trust that you know your contract for each life dimension. Contracts in the area of spirituality could be "I am a trusting, devotional, and compassionate servant of God," or "I am a responsible, focused, and committed spirit soul." Contracts for persons who have completed PACTs in the area of abundance include "I am clear, committed, and successful," and "I am a persistent, trusting, and flexible creator of wealth." Examples of relationship contracts include "I am present, open, authentic, and fearless," and "I am an honest, lovable, and confident man." Notice that contracts are expressed in the present tense—"I am" rather than "I would like to be" or "I want to be"—because our contracts are embedded in Be-Do-Have.

Contracting is not pretense. It is not "Fake it till you make it." It is a process that recognizes and honors our experience, without judgment, while applying clear intention to connect with our intrinsic spiritual nature. Our goals enrich our lives when they flow from our being, our deepest contract with ourselves.

Benjamin Franklin represents a fine example of integrating character development with goal attainment. At the age of twenty he identified thirteen virtues that he wished to exemplify. He committed to devoting close attention to one virtue each week, so that each year he completed a course in virtues four times. He monitored his progress with a careful charting system, with rows and columns for each virtue and day. In this way he would daily review and evaluate his progress, and this adherence became a foundation for his remarkable achievements.

For your Personal Achievement Compact select and write goals in terms that are specific, measurable, acceptable, realistic, and time-oriented.

S = Specific

M = Measurable

A = Acceptable

R = Realistic

T = Time-oriented

A goal such as, "I want to get good grades," is not specific. "I will score at least 90 percent on each of the next three math tests," on the other hand, is specific. A goal lacking specificity might be, "I want to be healthier." A specific goal would be, "My weight will be below 175 pounds within one month." It is important to state goals in terms that allow us to know whether we have achieved the objective. Expressing goals in measurable language is helpful for this. Measurable goals include:

"I will practice yoga at least half an hour per day, at least five days a week, for the next two months."

"I will drink a maximum of eight ounces of coffee per day for the next month."

"I will generate at least $40,000 of net sales per month for December, January and February."

'Acceptable' means *acceptable to you*. Do your goals align with your values? If so, then naturally you will be enlivened to achieve them. If we do not *own* our goals and actually embrace them, it will be difficult to generate sincere enthusiasm for them.

'Realistic' means *I am really going to do it*. We want our goals to be challenging and realistic. 'Realistic' is not a justification for complacency. Suppose that at present I generally rise in the morning between 7 and 8 a.m., and that it has been years since I have risen before 5 a.m. Realizing the benefits, spiritual and otherwise, of rising by 4 a.m., suppose that I then commit to rising by 4 a.m. every day for the rest of my life, beginning tomorrow. Perhaps I will succeed, but probably not. Maybe I will succeed for a few days, or a week or two, and then miss a day.

In setting goals it is important to set ourselves up for success. A challenging and realistic goal in the situation described above might be: "Beginning this week I will rise by 4 a.m. at least twice a week for the next month; then at least three times a week the month after that; then at least four times a week the month after that." I might endeavor to rise by 4 a.m. seven days a week starting now, and be realistically committed to doing so at least twice a week for the next month. Creating a foundation of successfully meeting our commitments—even if they seem relatively small—is a strong platform for building an accomplished and fulfilling life of integrity.

Also, this strategy is valuable for preventing a lapse from becoming a major relapse. Say that you are discarding an unwanted habit, such as smoking. Suppose that after smoking several packs per day for many years, you committed to stopping completely. Imagine that you were successful for ten days; then you smoked. It is possible that your broken commitment could contribute to a downward cycle of feeling useless, powerless and guilty, leading you to again smoke cigarettes and for a significant period of time abandon your plan to cease smoking. If instead your strategy was to *attempt* to completely stop, but *commit* to reduce by at least three cigarettes a day for the next twenty weeks, then if you did slip and smoked after ten days, you could feel encouraged that you were within the bounds of your commitment. Then the lapse could become an opportunity for examining what happened, learning more about yourself and revitalizing your enthusiasm to achieve your goal.

My purpose here is not to discourage you from setting lofty goals. Stretch yourself while incorporating the "realistic" principle and recognize that the learning curve is not always a vertical slope. With this in mind, consider also that a high goal is frequently easier to achieve than a low one. A low goal tends to exert low motivational force. This is why some of the most amazing things we accomplish actually seem relatively easy—because we were highly inspired.

Designate a timeline for your goal. Commit to a date by which you will achieve your result. This fosters a sense of urgency and helps to prevent procrastination.

Write a sentence or two describing why the goal is important for you, and how you will feel when you achieve it. This will support you in connecting with the *being* source of your Personal Achievement Compact and ensure that your goals are consistent with your highest purpose and values.

List concrete action steps you will take to achieve your goal. For example, if your goal is to complete an online course within 108 days, then the intermediary specific steps towards the goal may include a list of readings and assignments to be completed after one week, one month, and so on. If your goal is to be engaged in satisfying employment within three months, actions towards that goal might include preparing a quality resume within two weeks, and sending out at least thirty resumes within one month. If your intended accomplishment is to improve at least ten relationships in your life, then an accompanying action could be to do the *pulling the weeds* exercise with at least two relationships per week for the next two months, or to conduct empathic dialogues within your important relationships for at least two hours per week for one month.

PACT Examples

Sara rates her spiritual life at 5 out of 10. For Sara this area consists of several sub-areas, including meditation, rising early, gratitude, association with like-minded spiritualists, prayer, sanctifying her food, reading spiritual literature and listening to spiritual lectures. Though she doesn't feel fully satisfied in her practice within any of these areas, she is basically content in her reading, listening to lectures and visiting places of worship—and significantly unfulfilled in the other aspects. Sara envisions a 10 as follows: Rising by 5 a.m. every day and engaging in at least ninety minutes of meditation; visiting a place of worship where she feels safe, secure and spiritually enlivened at least once per week; meeting with persons whom she considers to be like-minded spiritualists on at least one additional occasion per week, for at least two hours; reserving at least fifteen minutes per day, apart from her morning meditation, for prayer; earnestly cultivating an attitude of gratitude towards God and toward the people in her life for the many blessings in her life; reading inspiring spiritual literature at least one hour per day; listening to spiritually-oriented lectures at least three hours per week.

Sara identifies her contract in this area as, "I am a trusting, disciplined and playful devotee of the divine spirit." She establishes the following as her compact with herself in the area of spiritual practice:

"I will rise by 5 a.m. at least one day per week, beginning this week. Beginning at the start of January 2008, I will rise by 5 a.m. at least two days per week, increasing this by one day per week per two months, so that by July 2008, I am rising by 5 a.m. at least five days per week. This is important for me to connect with my deepest sense of life purpose. Accomplishing this, I will feel vital and successful about my spiritual development.

"I will do meditation at least twenty minutes per day before 7 a.m., at least three days per week, beginning this week. Starting in January 2008, I will increase that to at least thirty minutes per day, at least three days per week. Beginning the first week of March, I will do this meditation for at least thirty minutes per day, for at least five days a week. Starting the first week of May, I will practice meditation for at least thirty minutes a day, at least five days a week, and in addition, at least sixty minutes a day before 7 a.m., at least one day a week. This is important for me to feel a vibrant, deep connection with my spirit and the divine spirit. Achieving this will provide me a feeling of security, joy and strength.

"I will read spiritually based literature at least half an hour per day, at least five days a week, beginning this week.

"I will listen to spiritually-oriented lectures at least three hours per week. This is important for me to remain connected with a state of elevated consciousness, and to be present and inspired in my daily dealings. By doing this, I will feel prepared to handle anything that arises in my life, and full of knowledge and wisdom that I can readily apply.

"Before taking rest at night, I will pray in a meditative mood to God for at least five minutes. I will begin this today. This is important for me to remember my position as a servant of the supreme, to be in clean consciousness while asleep, and to constantly enrich my link to God. By doing this I will feel the presence of God in my life.

"Beginning this week, I will express appreciation to at least three people in my life each week, for their qualities or behaviors that inspire me.

"Beginning this week I will write down at least ten blessings in my life, at least twice a week, for the next four weeks. Doing this will help me to be in a consciousness of gratitude, and to avoid spiritually draining emotions such as resentment and hostility. Through achieving these goals I will feel fortunate, thankful and blessed.

"I will arrange monthly meetings with like-minded spiritualists, either at my home or elsewhere, beginning this month. Beginning in March 2008, I will do this at least twice a month, until at least August 2008. Spiritual association is essential for me to maintain and expand my enthusiasm for spiritual practice. By achieving this goal I will feel excited to progress spiritually, and to share my realizations with others."

Envisioning herself achieving what she declares in this area of her PACT, Sara determines that within one month she would rate her spiritual practice at a 6, and after eight months it would be at least an 8, and maybe a 9.

Michael rates his area of Health/Fitness/Body at a 6. He is pleased with the fitness program that he has begun to implement, and there is much on which he wants to focus with regards to his relationship with eating and other health-related habits. For him, elements of a 10 include maintaining his daily thirty-minute workout; being a conscious eater by not consuming more than necessary; not eating after 8 p.m.; and regular visits to health professionals. His contract in the area of health is, "I am a conscientious, vital and valuable man." He states one of his goals in this area as follows: "For the next six months I will maintain a body weight of a maximum of 170 pounds."

Describing why this is important for him, Michael writes, "This is important for cultivating a consciousness of health, for preparing myself for the best use of my body in fulfilling my life purposes. By achieving this I will feel responsible that I am appropriately caring for my body. I will feel temperate, sober and vibrant."

In the area of relationships Michael's contract is: "I am a grateful, giving, and connected person." He currently rates this area as a 4. One quality on which he especially wants to focus is gratitude. He wants people close to him to know that he appreciates them, and he states his goal in terms of these concrete action steps. "I will express to at least three people per week specifically why I appreciate them and how they inspire me. I will do this beginning this week and continue for at least six weeks. At least twice per week I will write a journal entry about my experience doing this. This is important for me because I am perceived by my friends as harsh and critical, and I want to change this. Accomplishing this goal will enhance my self-worth, and will ensure that the quality of at least eighteen relationships is improved. This will be deeply satisfying, and will give me joy and fulfillment."

Michael's career contract is "I am a committed, enthusiastic and trusting giver." One of his goals is to complete the development of a new line of products by the end of the calendar year. He defines one of the action steps as, "I will devote at least ten hours per week for the next ten weeks to developing this line of products." Michael writes, "I intend to do this because this set of products will provide important value for clients, and will provide me with a sense of truly making a positive difference for people. Completing this project will be gratifying. I will feel productive, successful, useful, innovative and creative."

Take this opportunity to get clear on what you want—on what is vitally important for you. In the process of PACT-writing, many people realize that what they had assumed they wanted is not what they actually want in their lives. Maybe it was what they told themselves they *should* want, or what other people told them they should want.

This exercise may be a little disheartening, though clarifying what you do not want can be a gateway to discovering what is genuinely important for you. Towards the end of the courses I conduct, we include a process in which participants powerfully connect with clear intention. They practically experience "obstacles" that were preventing them from achieving a tangible goal, transforming them into mere *considerations* that they know they will handle on the way to accomplishing their objectives. In one course there was a woman who did not get the process. She recognized that she did not link up with the power of intention, as the others did. She was upset and angry with the process, with the other participants, with herself, with me. Then she realized that the reason she had not been able to switch from obstacle consciousness to consciousness in the result was because *the goal she chose for the process was not her own.* It was in fact a representation of how she was giving away her power of choice to others to determine what her life needed to look like. The goal that she had initially chosen for herself was revealed as a survival strategy, and she understood that this reflected how she had been living her life. This experience during the course led her to rediscover her authentic self.

This is a challenging process. Challenging ourselves and stretching our limits is how we grow. Certainly this requires effort, though this effort need not be experienced as a struggle. Struggle is a choice. Sometimes, in the endeavor to produce a result—internal or external—we can get absorbed in "trying." This trying can become a "looking good" strategy. We may become engrossed in convincing others, and ourselves, how hard we are trying. Strenuously trying is a different world than doing and accomplishing. With consciousness in the result, we achieve what we have declared in our PACT to be important to us, and we do not need to experience it as an arduous struggle. On top of the various challenges you set for yourself in your PACT, here is another one: Make it easy.

Insight and Action

*"You're more likely to act yourself into feelings
than feel yourself into action."*

—Jerome Bruner

Insight leads to action. For example, through the understanding gained by empathic presence, we are able to discern reality from illusion, connecting with core truths of our being—and then translate this into transformed action in all spheres of our life. Imbued with the qualities of our being, and applying clear intention and strategies for living, our behaviors assume a different character, leading to changed outcomes and experiences. Awareness of the rackets we played and the grungies we embraced inspires us to clean up our emotional and relational life, empowering our efforts and enabling us to live meaningfully.

Action in turn leads to insight. Often, transformation is based in action. Whatever insights we may or may not possess, effective action based on correct principles has the power to produce realization. Sometimes we may connect with our confidence and courage, leading to confident, courageous action. At other times we may not experience confidence and courage; perhaps we notice fear and insecurity. In such instances, we act anyway, driven not by fear but by our purpose, plan, and life strategy. For example, though we are not feeling particularly self-assured or secure, we determine, "I am going to raise my hand and express my opinion." Taking this action, we link with our natural confidence, assertiveness, and sense of self-value.

This purpose-driven life strategy does not depend on willpower, though of course willpower can be a helpful tool. We may find that sometimes our willpower is stronger, sometimes it is weaker. Clear intention to manifest the results within our PACTs transcends the ebb and flow of willpower, and moves us to the qualities we need in order to grow and achieve our goals.

Ideally, our Personal Achievement Compacts emerge from our *being*. Realization of self stimulates fulfilling activity. For those times when we are not experiencing connection with our contracts, we can be guided by the principle that "action leads to insight," and permit ourselves to live by the concrete vision that we have created in our PACTs.

Here I would like to differentiate between a vision and a dream. While dreams have their place, they become palpable visions when we are willing to set goals with tangible action steps. Genuine spiritual life is active. When our spirituality is fully uncovered and expressed, it is not that we become inactive. Rather, with self-realization our activity assumes full vitality, just as the actions of a diseased person acquire fullness and richness as he returns to health.

Our thoughts or belief systems generate our feelings, which engender our actions, and our actions determine our habits. Aristotle said that excellence is a habit, not an act. Commitment to excellence is commitment to auspicious habits, in speech, thought, and action. The PACT is a tool that allows us to integrate favorable habits and eliminate unhealthy ones. We are the managers of our lives. Just as the manager of an organization oversees various departments, we supervise diverse energies and activities such as money, spirituality, sexuality, eating, sleeping, communicating, and recreation. The PACT is an opportunity to take inventory of each life area on which you would like to focus, and become consciously responsible—the author of your life in every dimension. Cultivating effective habits throughout our lives, we build character and become the architect of our own destinies.

The PACT process is about accomplishing goals, and more essentially about developing favorable habits that form a foundation for achievements into the future. Think what it would mean for your experience of life to acquire four positive habits per year.

What would that look like ten years from now, in your *being, doing* and *having*—in each area of your life? Start now. Be in the habit of cultivating auspicious habits.

Insights translate more effectively into action when we share our goals with someone we trust. Consider finding a PACT buddy, or a team. With a team of others who are committed to supporting and challenging each other to fulfill their commitments and realize their life visions, your endeavors will become more potent.

Here is an action strategy to immediately move forward in a chosen area of your life, even if you are not prepared to write a full PACT with all of its elements. Select a life area and rate it from 0 to 10. Identify three things you could do, and are willing to commit to do, in the next two weeks to raise it by half a point. Choose a person to whom you will be accountable for reporting your progress and success in taking these actions, and follow through with your action steps.

A Life of Excellence

This program is especially designed for persons invested in a life of excellence, committed to living with urgency and not willing to settle for mediocrity. Writing a PACT is an opportunity to help you live in such a way that when you are ninety-nine and looking back on your life, you won't have regrets. As mentioned, this sense of urgency is not a frivolous life of momentary gratification, nor is it an anxiety-filled panic. It is an existence of full presence, where each moment counts, and where our intelligence and creativity are expressed in savoring every experience, and continually strengthening character and constructing a worthy future.

The agency of your PACT is a powerful instrument in transforming your relationship with fear—not allowing it to get in the way of being who you want to be, so that you can live the life you desire and create wonderful, exceptional results. This is particularly true for those who are tired of "potential." As University of Texas football coach Darrell Royal said, "'Potential' means you ain't done it yet."

Striving for excellence is distinct from demanding perfection. In seeking excellence we appreciate the perfection in the process of life itself, without the need to conform to some other definition of perfection. At each instant we can be present with the *rightness* of all things, embracing it, appreciating the wonder of it. At the same time, part of that perfection is that we are active, with dynamic self-determination. Our existence involves the innovative action that springs from our spiritual nature. While appreciating the completeness of Creation, our birthright is to continually enrich life, which includes ourselves and everyone with whom we come into contact. Endeavors to develop originate from inspiration and our natural tendency to grow, rather than from a place of neediness and scarcity. We are complete, whole and balanced, and we continually move with vitality towards a deeper experience of our spiritual qualities.

SATTVA AS A BASIS FOR SATISFACTION

The Vedic Personality Inventory (VPI) is provided in Appendix A at the back of this book (page 172). I recommend that you complete it periodically and note any changes in your *guna* profile. After taking it once and then applying spiritual principles for personal growth and living your contracts and PACT, retake the VPI after one month, three months and six months.

Studies have demonstrated that a *sattvic* lifestyle correlates with greater life satisfaction. For this reason I would like to present some additional practical guidance on actualizing *sattvic* consciousness. Different periods of the day are predominated by different modes of nature, and thus are most suited to particular types of activity. For example, late night hours are heavily influenced by *tamas*, and thus are generally when sleep is recommended. Early morning hours, especially the hour before sunrise, are distinctively *sattvic*, and are conducive for activities directly meant to enhance our spiritual consciousness.

As spiritual beings, a balanced and complete life includes cultivation of spirituality. Research has shown that spiritual practice correlates positively with better physical and mental health. Building spiritual habits entails scheduling time for spiritual practice, whether in the form of prayer, meditation, reading, attendance at congregational gatherings, silence, or time with nature. If spiritual life is relegated to something we do if there is time after responding to our emails or completing household chores, it won't happen.

A spiritual program that has worked for me for the past twenty-five years begins with rising early, by 4 or 5 a.m. This practice is itself invigorating. When I don't do it, I definitely feel the difference. Another staple of my spiritual diet is about ninety minutes of early morning meditation. I have found that mantra meditation is most effective for me. The senses are centered around the mind, and mantra chanting engages several senses and abilities, including hearing, speech, and touch (if the mantra is counted on beads such as a rosary). This makes it easier for our minds to focus on the vibration of the mantra. A mantra is a sound vibration that frees the mind ("mind" is derived from the first syllable of "mantra") from material entanglement, from the modes of *rajas* and *tamas*, and elevates our existence to the spiritual platform. We have explored how we create our life with our words, and how our mode of speech determines the atmosphere of our internal and relationship world. Attentive mantra chanting is another means to spiritualize our life through sound vibration.

Jill Bormann has conducted research on mantra meditation with various populations including military veterans. She describes meditative time with a mantra as a "Jacuzzi for the mind. It's something you can use to focus and calm yourself at a moment's notice, and it doesn't require money, it's non-toxic, it's inexpensive—a person just needs to practice it and make it a part of their lives." Jill and other researchers have found that regular recitation of selected mantras significantly helps manage psychological distress and increase life satisfaction. The veterans with whom she worked chose from a variety of mantras from diverse traditions, such as *Ave Maria* and *Om Shanti Rama*.

My personal favorite mantra for meditation is one of India's most beloved, *The Maha Mantra*, which goes *Hare Krishna, Hare Krishna, Krishna Krishna, Hare Hare / Hare Rama, Hare Rama, Rama Rama, Hare Hare*. Quantitative group and single-system research conducted by Dr. Neil Abell and myself has shown that chanting this mantra correlates with reduced stress and depression as well as with increased *sattvic* qualities such as peacefulness, fulfillment, emotional balance, mental clarity and sense of life purpose. Recitation of this mantra has been shown to be compatible with the realization of our spiritual identity, supporting us in connecting with the innermost stratum of the living soul.

People are sometimes surprised that I spend more than two hours per day in direct spiritual practice, thinking that this would not leave sufficient time for other endeavors and projects. My experience for over a quarter century is that if I don't devote at least two hours a day to activities such as chanting and reading spiritual literature that connects me directly to spirit and to the source of my existence, then I actually have less time and energy to do things. My spiritual practice vitalizes and strengthens me, fills me with a sense of urgency about life, of not wanting to waste a moment.

Also, spiritual practice, or *sadhana*, helps me to view and experience all my efforts in relation to God and spiritual development.

Each type of food has its characteristic mode. With reference to diet, *sattva* guna is complemented by foods that require a minimal amount of violence to obtain. Thus a vegetarian diet tends to increase our *sattvic* consciousness. There is a Buddhist aphorism— *ahimsa paramo dharma*—nonviolence is the highest virtue. After witnessing the slaughter of an animal, Leo Tolstoy wrote, "This is dreadful!...that a man suppresses in himself, unnecessarily, the highest spiritual capacity—that of sympathy towards living creatures like himself..." To help us cultivate empathy and actualize refined spiritual consciousness, awareness of what we consume is vital.

We are influenced by the people we associate with, perhaps more than we realize. Developing *sattvic* habits and refining our character is facilitated by developing close relations with others who are similarly committed to the cultivation of self-realization. If we want to grow, to play a big game with our lives, it helps to surround ourselves with people who will support and challenge us to be the best that we can be. These are true friends who will not sell us short and who actively encourage us to live in excellence. Just as a medical student will closely associate with other medical students to help achieve his or her goal, just as a businessperson interacts with other businesspeople, so an aspiring spiritualist seeks out the affiliation of like-minded spiritualists.

Other aspects of our environment are also important to consider in fulfilling our PACTs and nurturing *sattvic* mindfulness. Suppose, for instance, that we set a goal of regulating our eating. To assist us in achieving this we will naturally attend to our surroundings. If I want to reduce sweets, it will help that I do not keep delectable sweets in front of my face. If my goal is to rise early, then I know I will have a better chance of accomplishing this if I am not watching television at midnight.

Let us remember that the commitments in our PACTs, and the various recommended structures for *sattvic* living, are meant to serve our life purpose. We utilize them to achieve our heartfelt aims, not to be bound in servitude to these structures. We "get to" fulfill our objectives and live an inspired, commitment-driven life of intention.

Regulation or structure may appear limiting. Actually, when intelligently applied, a regulative framework is freeing. For example, I may think, "Rules constrain me. I am a free person. That is why I drive through red lights, and pay no attention to speed limit signs or lines on the road." In this case, my sense of so-called freedom will result in much greater restraints, perhaps in prison or the hospital. Just as codes governing the road provide an environment for us to arrive safely at our destination, through our PACTs we design structures that assist us in uplifting our consciousness and accomplishing our true purpose.

The *Bhagavad Gita* explains the concept of "regulative principles of freedom." Through carefully nurturing *sattvic* habits, we become free of the effects of *rajas* and *tamas*, and our innate spiritual qualities flourish. *Guna* means "mode," and it also means "rope." We are entangled in material consciousness by the *gunas*, or ropes. A tangle of knots is unsnarled by pulling on the correct rope, and the knots become even more enmeshed by pulling the wrong rope. Nurturing *sattva guna* is pulling the rope that will extricate us from the Gordian knot of material consciousness.

In establishing goals for our PACT, let us consider whether the goals will elevate our consciousness. Will they genuinely enhance our lives, and situate us more deeply in spirit?

CELEBRATE SUCCESSES

The adventure of spiritual growth and self-development is likely to be filled with peaks and valleys, plateaus and slopes. Acknowledging your successes and celebrating your accomplishments is a valuable habit. This doesn't just refer to "big" achievements; Many people have found the practice of listing five successes per day to be a powerful habit that augments healthy, enlivened, and productive perspectives. This habit is simply to write down at the end of the day five successes, in any area of life, that you accomplished during that day. This is another helpful structure to help you to be on contract and fulfill your PACT goals. Here are some examples of *five successes* lists:

1. Spent satisfying hour in conversation and enjoyable activity with my son;
2. Opened two new sales accounts;
3. Walked three miles;
4. Controlled anger when provoked by coworker;
5. Filed papers on my desk.

1. Cleared 15 minutes during the day for quiet meditation;
2. Responded to five letters;
3. Collected overdue accounts;
4. Ate moderately;
5. Sent manuscript to magazine.

Recognizing our achievements is a salutary practice for steadily and expertly navigating the roller coaster journey of self-realization.

SERVICE AND
SELF-DEVELOPMENT

In my experience with thousands of coaching clients and seminar participants, and with myself, I have found that significant breakthroughs in transformation and self-empowerment are consistently related to service. Spiritual development is intrinsically connected with unlocking our gifts so that the totality of our qualities is available to the world. Cultivation of spiritual consciousness and writing and fulfilling our PACTs are not exercises in self-absorption. This is a process of self-reflection and personal realization, a commitment to unfolding our capacity for giving and for affecting a positive difference in the world.

Being mission-oriented intrinsically helps us to resolve internal and relational conflicts and to manifest our God-given abilities. With consciousness in an admirable and spiritually oriented result, we will be better empathic listeners, accept responsibility for our lives, act from a deeper sense of honesty with ourselves and others, and be more attentive to being in integrity and honoring agreements.

As you formulate your PACT, I encourage you to focus on the active service nature of the self. Within your PACT it is natural to include objectives related to self-care. From a *sattvic* perspective this is essential for your constant motion towards balance. An attitude of service to others recognizes that they are part of the supreme spirit. You are too. Attending to and nourishing yourself is an opportunity to care for a creation of God. We invest in ourselves so that the entirety of our being is available to give to others, to be fully present in each interaction, living with vivid urgency in connection with the divine.

Martin Luther King, Jr. said, "Greatness comes through serving others." Review your PACT with this principle in mind. The point is not to be "great" in an ostentatious sense, but rather to be deep in character through dedicated and purely motivated service. Through willingness to accept responsibility for concerns of true significance, by serving that which is bigger than yourself, your cares and anxieties assume a different appearance. In service to that which is grander than self-centered or extended selfish activities, whatever weighty internal issues and weeds in the heart that we are meant to deal with in this lifetime rise to the surface. Uplifting service provides an opportunity to address all that is within, a chance to clear the path for complete spiritual expression. As Holocaust survivor, writer, and founder of logotherapy Victor Frankl expressed it, "Nothing is more likely to help a person overcome or endure troubles than the consciousness of having a task in life."

Service is necessarily based on empathy. To genuinely serve, we need to know the desires and needs of the person whom we are serving. Otherwise our endeavors to serve will be concocted, more self-serving than authentically caring about others. In any field of endeavor, service entails an ability to listen, and a commitment to understand. Truly unconditional service is endearing. Social worker Harry Hopkins was the most trusted advisor of President Franklin D. Roosevelt. Extraordinarily influential, Hopkins was also controversial and aroused fierce criticism. In January 1941, Wendell Willkie visited Roosevelt and asked him, "Why do you keep Hopkins so close to you? You surely must realize that people distrust him and resent his influence." Roosevelt replied, "Someday you may well be sitting here where I am now as president of the United States. And when you are, you'll be looking at that door over there and knowing that practically everybody who walks through it wants something out of you. You'll learn what a lonely job this is and discover the need for somebody like Harry Hopkins who asks for nothing except to serve you."

Service is the basis of leadership—true leadership, not as a position or title, but as a choice, a way of being. Each of us is meant to be a leader, whether in our families, communities, offices, or on the world stage. Spiritual principles of personal growth—personified through a service-oriented PACT—provide a structure for a life of leadership, of being an inspiring model for everyone with whom we come into contact.

Appendix A

The Vedic Personality Inventory

1: Very Strongly Disagree 2: Strongly Disagree
3: Somewhat Disagree 4: Neutral 5: Somewhat Agree
6: Strongly Agree 7: Very Strongly Agree

		1	2	3	4	5	6	7
1.	I am straightforward in my dealings with other people.	☐	☐	☐	☐	☐	☐	☐
2.	I have very little interest in spiritual understanding.	☐	☐	☐	☐	☐	☐	☐
3.	I am satisfied with my life.	☐	☐	☐	☐	☐	☐	☐
4.	Fruits and vegetables are among my favorite foods.	☐	☐	☐	☐	☐	☐	☐
5.	All living entities are essentially spiritual.	☐	☐	☐	☐	☐	☐	☐
6.	In conducting my activities, I do not consider traditional wisdom.	☐	☐	☐	☐	☐	☐	☐
7.	I often act without considering the future consequences of my actions.	☐	☐	☐	☐	☐	☐	☐
8.	I usually feel discontented with life.	☐	☐	☐	☐	☐	☐	☐
9.	I become happy when I think about the material assets that I possess.	☐	☐	☐	☐	☐	☐	☐
10.	I am good at using willpower to achieve goals.	☐	☐	☐	☐	☐	☐	☐

11. I enjoy spending time in bars. ❏ ❏ ❏ ❏ ❏ ❏ ❏

12. Cleanliness is very important to me. ❏ ❏ ❏ ❏ ❏ ❏ ❏

13. Others say that my intelligence is very sharp. ❏ ❏ ❏ ❏ ❏ ❏ ❏

14. I often feel depressed. ❏ ❏ ❏ ❏ ❏ ❏ ❏

15. I often put off or delay my responsibilities. ❏ ❏ ❏ ❏ ❏ ❏ ❏

16. I greatly admire materially successful people. ❏ ❏ ❏ ❏ ❏ ❏ ❏

17. When I speak, I really try not to irritate others. ❏ ❏ ❏ ❏ ❏ ❏ ❏

18. I believe life is over when the body dies. ❏ ❏ ❏ ❏ ❏ ❏ ❏

19. I often feel helpless. ❏ ❏ ❏ ❏ ❏ ❏ ❏

20. I enjoy foods with strong tastes. ❏ ❏ ❏ ❏ ❏ ❏ ❏

21. I am constantly dissatisfied with my position in life. ❏ ❏ ❏ ❏ ❏ ❏ ❏

22. Having possessions is very important to me. ❏ ❏ ❏ ❏ ❏ ❏ ❏

23. When things are tough, I often bail out. ❏ ❏ ❏ ❏ ❏ ❏ ❏

24. I often feel like a victim. ❏ ❏ ❏ ❏ ❏ ❏ ❏

25. I feel that my knowledge is always increasing. ❏ ❏ ❏ ❏ ❏ ❏ ❏

26. I prefer city nightlife to a walk in the forest. ❏ ❏ ❏ ❏ ❏ ❏ ❏

27. My sex life is a major source of happiness. ❏ ❏ ❏ ❏ ❏ ❏ ❏

28. I take guidance from higher ethical and moral laws before I act. ❏ ❏ ❏ ❏ ❏ ❏ ❏

29. I enjoy intoxicating substances (including coffee, cigarettes and alcohol). ❏ ❏ ❏ ❏ ❏ ❏ ❏

30. I often feel greedy. ❏ ❏ ❏ ❏ ❏ ❏ ❏

31. I become greatly distressed when things don't work out for me. ❏ ❏ ❏ ❏ ❏ ❏ ❏

32. I am often angry. ❏ ❏ ❏ ❏ ❏ ❏ ❏

33. I often feel fearful. ❏ ❏ ❏ ❏ ❏ ❏ ❏

34. I do not have doubts about my responsibilities in life. ❏ ❏ ❏ ❏ ❏ ❏ ❏

35. I often feel emotionally unbalanced. ❏ ❏ ❏ ❏ ❏ ❏ ❏

36. I enjoy eating meat. ❏ ❏ ❏ ❏ ❏ ❏ ❏

37. I am self-controlled. ❏ ❏ ❏ ❏ ❏ ❏ ❏

38. I am very dutiful. ❏ ❏ ❏ ❏ ❏ ❏ ❏

39. When I give to charity, I often do so grudgingly. ❏ ❏ ❏ ❏ ❏ ❏ ❏

40. Self-realization is not important to me. ❏ ❏ ❏ ❏ ❏ ❏ ❏

41. I often feel dejected. ❏ ❏ ❏ ❏ ❏ ❏ ❏

42. I carry out my responsibilities regardless of whether I meet with success or failure. ❏ ❏ ❏ ❏ ❏ ❏ ❏

43. I often neglect my responsibilities to my family. ❏ ❏ ❏ ❏ ❏ ❏ ❏

44. I am easily affected by the joys and sorrows of life. ☐ ☐ ☐ ☐ ☐ ☐ ☐

45. I often whine. ☐ ☐ ☐ ☐ ☐ ☐ ☐

46. Regardless of what I acquire or achieve, I have an uncontrollable desire to obtain more. ☐ ☐ ☐ ☐ ☐ ☐ ☐

47. I am currently struggling with an addiction, physical or psychological, to some type of intoxicant (including caffeine, cigarettes, and alcohol). ☐ ☐ ☐ ☐ ☐ ☐ ☐

48. I often envy others. ☐ ☐ ☐ ☐ ☐ ☐ ☐

49. My job is a source of anxiety. ☐ ☐ ☐ ☐ ☐ ☐ ☐

50. I never think about giving up my wealth and position for a simpler life. ☐ ☐ ☐ ☐ ☐ ☐ ☐

51. It often happens that those things that brought me happiness later become the source of my suffering. ☐ ☐ ☐ ☐ ☐ ☐ ☐

52. I often feel mentally imbalanced. ☐ ☐ ☐ ☐ ☐ ☐ ☐

53. I don't have much will power. ☐ ☐ ☐ ☐ ☐ ☐ ☐

54. I often neglect my responsibilities to my friends. ☐ ☐ ☐ ☐ ☐ ☐ ☐

55. I often act violently towards others. ☐ ☐ ☐ ☐ ☐ ☐ ☐

56. I am good at controlling my senses and emotions. ☐ ☐ ☐ ☐ ☐ ☐ ☐

VPI Scoring Key

Sattva — 1, 3, 4, 5, 10, 12, 13, 17, 25, 28, 34, 37, 38, 42, 56
Rajas — 8, 9, 16, 18, 20, 21, 22, 23, 26, 27, 30, 31, 39, 44, 46, 48, 49, 50, 51
Tamas — 2, 6, 7, 11, 14, 15, 19, 24, 29, 32, 33, 35, 36, 40, 41, 43, 45, 47, 52, 53, 54, 55

Scoring Instructions: Add all the responses for a *guna*, then divide this sum by the total possible score for the *guna*. This will give the *guna* score in the form of a percentage. Then, to obtain a standardized score for a *guna*, add up the three *guna* percentage scores and divide the total into the *guna* percentage scores. The three standardized scores form the *guna* profile for a person.

Example:

For the 15 *sattva* items a respondent scores 60, or an average of 4.0. This converts to a *guna* percentage score of 57.14 percent (60/105 or 4/7).

For the 19 *rajas* items a respondent scores 57, or an average of 3.0. This converts to a *guna* percentage score of 42.86 percent (57/133 or 3/7).

For the 22 *tamas* items a respondent scores 55, or an average of 2.5. This converts to a *guna* percentage score of 35.71 percent (55/154 or 2.5/7).

The sum of the three *guna* percentage scores is 57.14 + 42.86 + 35.71 = 135.71

The standardized *sattva* score is 57.14/135.71 = 42.10 percent

The standardized *rajas* score is 42.86/135.71 = 31.58 percent

The standardized *tamas* score is 35.71/135.71 = 26.31 percent

Appendix B

Responses to Exercises and Additional Transformative Communication Processes

In this appendix are supplemental exercises for enriching your capacity to create sacred space. In the safe interpersonal environment created by applying the principles and skills described in this section, we feel secure enough to express ourselves at a deep level of honesty. In an atmosphere devoid of roadblocks to communication and imbued with genuine desire to understand, we are supported, courageous, and inspired to express what is authentically true for us.

Here are responses to Exercises 1 and 2, found in the *Transformative Communication: Creating Sacred Space* section of the book.

Responses to Exercise 1:

1. Response A — Accurate empathy; Response B — Interpreting, Psychoanalyzing, Blaming, Criticizing; Response C — Cliché/platitude, Reassurance; Response D — Ordering, Analysis.

2. Response A — Name-calling; Response B — Accurate empathy; Response C — Prophecy, Warning; Response D — Lecturing, Moralizing.

3. Response A — Praise, Denying/Minimizing, Diverting; Response B — Accurate empathy; Response C — Blaming, Criticizing, Accusing; Response D — Preaching, Moralizing.

Responses to Exercise 2:

1. "Don't be ridiculous. You have so much to live for." [*Denying; Minimizing; Invalidating*]

   "You are feeling down and deeply discouraged because of the diagnosis." [*Empathic response*]

2. "You should immediately go in and speak directly with him. And I think you should just apologize about the reports and stay up late and complete them today." [*Advice; Ordering*]

   "You're apprehensive because you know you're not performing well." [*Empathic response*]

3. "You're so smart, and humble too." [*Praise*]

   "You're excited and surprised because you thought you failed the exam, and you received a high grade." [*Empathic response*]

4. "You need to decide soon, or life will pass you by." [*Warning*]

   "You're feeling confused about what to do because you have different options and people are giving varying advice." [*Empathic response*]

5. "I'm sure everything will be fine for you." [*Reassurance*]

   "You're feeling unfulfilled because you know you can do more with your life." [*Empathic response*]

Additional Exercises to
Enhance Empathic Ability

Exercise 1

For a few days observe how frequently you use empathic under-standing in your communication style. After a few days, without being inauthentic or preoccupied with the effort, increase your use of reflective listening. Notice the impact of your use of empathy on others and on the process of communication.

Exercise 2

Identify three interpersonal scenarios in your life. Imagine you are making a statement about something that is troubling you, and then, taking the role of the person you are speaking with, write three responses, using different roadblocks. Use the roadblocks to which you are most susceptible. Consider the effect of the responses, and identify how each roadblock makes you feel. Then, formulate an empathic response for each scenario. To clarify, for each scenario you will formulate three roadblock responses, and one empathic response.

Example: A course participant approaching her teacher about the behavior of a third person.

> "I really think you need to speak with him one-on-one. I think he's doing things that are not conducive for a healthy lifestyle."
>
> *Roadblock response 1:* "I think that you should be careful about telling me what to do, or else you may be the one I will want to talk to." [*Threatening, Warning*]
>
> *Roadblock response 2:* "Oh, he'll be okay. Don't worry." [*False reassurance*]
>
> *Roadblock response 3:* "You just go and tell him what you think and how he has to change!" [*Ordering*]

Empathic response: "It is distressing for you to see that he is doing things that may be harmful for him. I can see that you're concerned about him, and you'd like me to speak with him."

After reviewing each response, consider how you would feel after receiving it. For the empathic responses you formulate, include reflection of content and emotion. For instance, in the example above, "It is distressing for you" is a reflection of feeling and "he is doing things that may be harmful" is a reflection of content.

Exercise 3

Conduct a written self-empathy dialogue. Select a challenge in your life. This could be related to your interpersonal style or a trait of your personality, or an issue connected with your career, health, relationships, spirituality or any life area. Use the skill of empathic reflection to help yourself explore this subject. Connect with yourself and stay with the mirroring process, without road-blocks or a suggested action plan. Here is an example involving a case manager at a family services center.

Self: I really don't know if I should continue at this job. I've been here for three years, and I've always appreciated it. I didn't expect this would happen, but I'm thinking it's time to leave. I'm questioning why I'm here.

Response to self: You've been satisfied at this job for three years. Now it's a surprise to yourself that you're not feeling fulfilled, and you are seriously thinking to leave.

Self: Yes. I'm still helping the families, doing some brief counseling, making referrals, and they are grateful for my efforts. I just don't get a sense that I'm making a substantial difference.

Response: You know that your endeavors are valuable for your clients. Still, you're feeling somewhat empty. You're not contributing to people to the degree that you sense you're capable of. This is frustrating.

Self: Yes, empty and frustrated. That's what's going on for me. I know I didn't feel this way when I started here. Now I feel like I'm cheating myself, and them. It's a struggle to come to work in the morning.

Response: You're definitely not satisfied there. And it sounds like you're at a point where you can't deny this. It's difficult to face each day at work. Something has changed from when you began at this position. You've shifted, and though it's a challenge to acknowledge it, it seems that it's time for you to move on.

Self: That does seem undeniable. I've grown out of this job. But I'm comfortable here, and where will I go? What will I do?

Response: You seem clear that it's time to leave this job. At the same time you're feeling insecure about that decision. You're afraid of what lies ahead and of how you'll earn a living. You're wondering what's in store for you.

Bibliography and Suggested Books
for Further Exploration

Buber, Martin. *Between Man and Man*. New York: Routledge Classic, 2002.

Carlson, R. *Don't Sweat the Small Stuff...and It's All Small Stuff*. New York: Hyperion, 1977.

Canfield, Jack, and Hansen, Mark Victor. *Chicken Soup for the Teenage Soul III: More Stories of Life, Love and Learning*. Deerfield: Health Communication, Inc., 2000.

Carson, Rick. *Taming Your Gremlin (Revised Edition): A Surprisingly Simple Method for Getting Out of Your Own Way*. New York: HarperCollins Publishers, 2003.

Chandler, Alfred D., Jr. *Scale and Scope: The Dynamics of Industrial Capitalism*. Boston: Harvard University Press, 1994.

Ciszek, Walter J., Flaherty, Daniel L. *He Leadeth Me*. New York: Doubleday Publishing, 1973.

Corning, Peter. *Nature's Magic: Synergy in Evolution and the Fate of Humankind*. Cambridge: University Press, 2003.

Covey, Stephen, R. *The Seven Habits of Highly Effective People: Powerful Lessons in Personal Change*. New York: Free Press, 1989.

Echterling, Lennis G. *Thriving!: A Manual for Students in the Helping Professions*. Boston: Houghton Mifflin, 2002.

Egan, G. *The Skilled Helper: A Systematic Approach to Effective Helping*. Pacific Grove, California: Brooks/Cole Publishing Company, 1990.

Egan, G. *The Skilled Helper: A Model for Systematic Helping and Interpersonal Relating*. Belmont, California: Wadsworth Publishing Company, 1975.

Eker, T. H. *Secrets of the Millionaire Mind: Mastering the Inner Game of Wealth*. New York: HarperBusiness, 2005.

Ende, Michael. *Momo*. New York: Penguin Group, 1984.

Epictetus. Translated by Wentworth Higginson, Thomas. *The Works Of Epictetus: Consisting Of His Discourses, In Four Books, The Enhiridion And Fragments*. Whitefish: Kessinger Publishing, LLC, 2007.

Faber, A. and Mazlish, E. *Liberated Parents, Liberated Children: Your Guide to a Happier Family.* New York: Avon Books, Inc., 1990.

Faber, A. and Mazlish, E. *How to Talk So Kids Will Listen & Listen So Kids Will Talk.* New York: Avon Books, 1980.

Frankl, Viktor Emil. *The Doctor and the Soul: From Psychotherapy to Logotherapy.* New York: Vintage Books, 1973.

Gazda, G. M. *Human Relations Development: A Manual for Educators.* Allyn and Bacon, 1998.

Goleman, Daniel. *Working with Emotional Intelligence.* New York: Bantam Books, 1998.

Grason, S. *Journalution: Journaling to Awaken Your Inner Voice, Heal Your Life, and Manifest Your Dreams.* Novato, California: New World Library, 2005.

Hart, Sura, and Kindle, Hodson Victoria. *The Compassionate Classroom: Relationship Based Teaching and Learning.* Encinitas, California: PuddleDancer Press, 2004.

Hendricks, Gay and Kathlyn. *Conscious Loving.* New York: Bantam Books.

Hendrix, Harville. *Getting the Love You Want: A Guide for Couples.* New York: Henry Holt and Company, LLC., 1998.

Hesse, Herman. *The Glass Bead Game: (Magister Ludi).* New York: Henry Holt and Company, 1990.

Hesse, Herman. *Siddhartha.* New York: New Directions Publishing Corporation, 1951.

The Holy Bible: Containing the Old and New Testaments. Cambridge: University of Cambridge Press, 1881.

Hill, Napoleon. *Think and Grow Rich.* Radford: Wilder Publication, 2007.

Jolley, Willie. *It Only Takes a Minute to Change Your Life!* New York: St. Martin's Press, 1997.

Kierkegaard, Søren. *The Sickness Unto Death.* London: Penguin Group, 1989.

McGraw, Philip, C. *Self Matters: Creating Your Life from the Inside Out.* New York: Simon and Schuster, Inc., 2001.

McGraw, Philip, C. *Life Strategies: Doing What Works, Doing What Matters.* New York: Hyperion, 1999.

Monks of New Skete. *In the Spirit of Happiness*. Cambridge: Back Bay, 2001.

Prabhupada, A. C. Bhaktivedanta Swami. *Bhagavad-Gita As It Is*. Los Angeles: Bhaktivedanta Book Trust, Classic Reprint 2001.

Prabhupada, A. C. Bhaktivedanta Swami. *Srimad Bhagavatam*. Los Angeles: Bhaktivedanta Book Trust, 1987.

Prabhupada, A. C. Bhaktivedanta Swami. *The Nectar Of Instruction*. Los Angeles: Bhaktivedanta Book Trust, 1975.

Prochaska, J. O., Morcross, J. C., and DiClemente, C. C. *Changing for Good: A Revolutionary Six-Stage Program for Overcoming Bad Habits and Moving Your Life Positively Forward*. New York: Avon Books, 1994.

Rosenberg, M. B. *Nonviolent Communication: A Language of Life*. Encinitas, California: PuddleDancer Press, 2005.

Sherwood, R. E. *Roosevelt and Hopkins: An Intimate History*. New York: Harper and Brothers, 1948.

Sheth, Jagdish, Sobel, Andrew. *Clients for Life: How Great Professionals Develop Breakthrough Relationships*. New York: Simon & Shuster, 2000.

Tolstoy, Leo. Translated by Maude Aylmer. *Essays and Letters*. Oxford: Oxford University Press, 1911.

Twain, Mark. *The Adventures of Tom Sawyer*. New York: Grosset and Dunlap, Inc., 1974.

Whitworth, L., Kimsey-House, H., and P. Sandahl. *Co-Active Coaching*. Mountain View, California: Davies-Black Publishing, 1998.

Wilber, K. *Integral Spirituality: A Startling New Role for Religion in the Modern and Postmodern World*. Boston: Integral Books, 2006.

Zannos, Susan. *Chester Carlton and the Development of Xerography*. Hockessin: Mitchell Lane Publishers, Inc., 2002.

About the Author

David B. Wolf, Ph.D., has more than twenty-five years of professional experience in a variety of social and mental health service fields, including counselor training, medical social work and children and family counseling. In 1998 he started the Association for the Protection of Children, an international child protection agency, and served as its director for six years. As part of his doctoral studies he developed the Vedic Personality Inventory (VPI), a personality assessment tool based on Vedic psychology.

Dr. Wolf founded Satvatove Institute (www.satvatove.org), a nonprofit organization based in north Florida dedicated to educating people in transformative communication and principles of spiritual empowerment. He has conducted Satvatove seminars in more than a dozen countries, and has coached and counseled thousands of people, groups and organizations. Additionally, he has developed the training program for Satvatove transformative communication specialists and life coaches. David lives with his wife and two children in Florida.

Satvatove Institute

Satvatove's programs provide spiritually based personal and group transformation through empowered communication, courageous introspection and purposeful action. Core programs include the Foundational Life Skills/Personal Transformation Seminar, the Advanced Seminar Experience and the Life Mastery Program. Satvatove's workshops and seminars utilize the experiential learning model, providing each student the opportunity to integrate and master principles of self-development and skills of transformative communication. For more information, visit www.satvatove.com, www.transformativecommunication.org, or access the Vedic Personality Inventory (VPI) online at www. VedicPersonality.org. Excerpts from Dr. Wolf's dissertation on the effects of mantra chanting, and articles from the Satvatove newsletter are available at www.yedaveda.net. Send comments and questions to comments@satvatove.com.

Acknowledgments

Associates who are aware that I've completed the manuscript for this book sometimes ask "How long did it take you to write it?" I find this a difficult question. Should I respond in terms of hours in front of the keyboard, months from the first sentence of the initial draft till the completion of the editing process, or years from the concrete conception of the project to the writing of these acknowledgements?

This volume has been a process, and I'd like to recognize persons who have been especially influential for me in this process. Since we need to begin somewhere, I'll begin in 1979 when my sister Carol Wolf encouraged, or perhaps persuaded, me to participate in the Lifespring Trainings developed by John Hanley, Sr. These personal growth programs are an early inspiration for many of the transformational principles and methodologies described in *Relationships That Work: The Power of Conscious Living.*

My personal realizations from these seminars moved me, over a period of about two years, to change majors from engineering to psychology. In line with this shift I entered the training program at On Drugs, Inc., a short-term and crisis-intervention counseling center in State College, Pennsylvania. My experience there as a trainee, counselor and trainer of counselors serves as a major influence for the communication principles and skills included in this book.

Along with my study of psychology I developed an interest in spiritual science, and began reading in that field. The writings of A. C. Bhaktivedanta Swami have been especially enlightening for me, and form the basis for the spiritual principles contained in these pages.

I'd like to recognize other writers and seminar facilitators who have contributed to the inspiration for this book. These include Steve Caron, Stephen Covey, Richard Carlson, Richard Carson, Gerard Egan, Harv Eker, Adele Faber, George Gazda, Kathlyn and Gay Hendricks, Harville Hendrix, Lucinda Lawton, Elaine Mazlish, Phil McGraw, Marshall Rosenberg, Jagdish Sheth, Andrew Sobel, Laura Whitworth and Ken Wilber.

I offer my appreciation to my wife Miriam, for her support in this project and for giving me the priceless gift of space to write this book, and to our children, Sita and Abhi, for inspiring me with their spirit and vitality to live the principles of Transformative Communication. My gratitude is also extended to my parents, Jules and Gert, for their complete dedication to creating an environment and culture conducive for my growth and full expression.

To the participants in the Satvatove programs over the years: I am honored by the trust you've shown to invite me into your lives. Your courage and commitment to live your best life has been steady encouragement for me to continue to offer Transformative Communication to the world, including the attempt of this book. I thank Marie Glasheen for her vision, support, and belief in me that has been a driving force in the unfolding of this book and the Satvatove programs. She has been a true and reliable friend and colleague for many years and I feel fortunate that she serves as Managing Director of Savatove Institute.

With appreciation I recognize the efforts of Neil Abell, Caitlin Barreira, Peter Burwash, Miriam Galarza, Bhakti-lata Gauthier, Naveen Khurana, and William Ogle for their valuable comments and insights during various phases of the development of the manuscript. I am deeply grateful to Patricia L. Harrison and Manjari Gauthier for their aesthetic contributions to this project.

I am very grateful to Arjuna Van der Kooij for his skill and patience in editing, and for encouraging and challenging me throughout the process of writing. Also to the group at Mandala Publishing and Palace Press I extend my thanks for their commitment and efforts to make this book possible.

"Relationships That Work: The Power of Conscious Living *is straightforward and sublime, practical and profound. David's book inspires us to full expression in our lives."*

—Sandy Grason, author of *Journalution: Journaling to Awaken Your Inner Voice, Heal Your Life and Manifest Your Dreams*

"Dr. Wolf has been able to explain not only who we are but he has also given us some paths to elevate our consciousness and help us on our way to a more productive, happy existence."

—Peter Burwash, author of *The Key to Great Leadership, Total Health* and *Improving the Landscape of Your Life*

"Dr. Wolf's Relationships That Work: The Power of Conscious Living *helps readers connect mind, body and spirit in a way that makes sense."*

—Jeff Kaplan, Ph.D., Master Certified Coach, Director, Dr. Jeff Kaplan & Associates

"Dr. Wolf has provided us with a clear, accessible summary of key principles that have guided his life and work for decades.... By encouraging us to reflect, reframe, and act with clear intention, he gently directs us down a path to greater understanding of the opportunities and options available in both personal and professional relations."

—Neil Abell, Associate Professor, College of Social Work, Florida State University

"[A] must read for anyone seeking self-understanding and better communication with those they care most about."

—E. Burke Rochford Jr., Professor of Sociology and Religion, Middlebury College

"As a practitioner for over twenty-five years, this personal growth guide has given me new and practical suggestions for guiding clients to better relationships with self, others and one's sense of spirituality."

—Carol Wittman, Ph.D., Private Practice Psychotherapist

"As you read this book you are likely to have profound insights into your own psyche that will help you achieve a better understanding of yourself and how to improve your life."

—Miriam Mendoza, Teacher, New York City Public Schools

"Dr. Wolf gives the reader a powerful context and practical set of tools to effectively and passionately live and love life to its fullest on all levels: the intellectual, physical, emotional and spiritual."

—Steven R. Caron, Entrepreneur and Life Transformation Coach